METAMORPHOSIS

ASTONISHING INSECT TRANSFORMATIONS

METAMORPHOSIS

ASTONISHING INSECT TRANSFORMATIONS

Written and photographed by
RUPERT SOSKIN

B L O O M S B U R Y

LONDON · NEW DELHI · NEW YORK · SYDNEY

To my grandson Finley
who arrived in this world
around the same time
as a number of the creatures
within these pages.

Bloomsbury Natural History

An imprint of Bloomsbury Publishing Plc

50 Bedford Square   1385 Broadway
London   New York
WC1B 3DP   NY 10018
UK   USA

www.bloomsbury.com
BLOOMSBURY and the Diana logo are trademarks of Bloomsbury Publishing Plc
First published 2015

British Library Cataloguing-in-Publication Data

A catalogue record for this book is available from the British Library.

ISBN: HB: 978-1-4081-7375-6

10 9 8 7 6 5 4 3 2 1

Designed by Nicola Liddiard, Nimbus Design
Printed in China

To find out more about our authors and books visit www.bloomsbury.com.
Here you will find extracts, author interviews, details of forthcoming events
and the option to sign up for our newsletters.

FOREWORD

Insects are all around us. They are much more numerous and have a greater collective biomass than any other multi-cellular life form on the planet. They have been on Earth for hundreds of millions of years – they were the first creatures to leave the sea for dry land and the first to take to the skies above. They are essential to the continued and healthy functioning of terrestrial and freshwater ecosystems, and yet we pay them little heed apart from spending vast sums of money on combating pest species.

Like all arthropods, insects have a jointed exoskeleton covering the whole of the outside of their bodies. This waterproof, protective layer, known as cuticle, is secreted by an epidermal layer of cells. As insects grow from egg to adult, the cuticle needs to be shed periodically. When moulting occurs, the old cuticle is shed, revealing a new one beneath that is then expanded and hardened.

This technically brilliant and thoroughly readable book is a study and celebration of these incredible transformations. To photograph the process of moulting needs superhuman patience and the inquiring mind of a scientist. To capture them in all their splendour needs the eye of an artist. Most people know that caterpillars turn into butterflies and maggots into flies, but how many have taken the time to record the process in all its beauty and complexity?

Rupert Soskin has the vision and all-consuming passion needed to take a subject so widespread and yet so little noticed and make it accessible and engaging – *Metamorphosis* will change the way you look at insects.

Dr George McGavin

A larva of the bagworm moth *Psyche casta* teeters along a single filament of rope, looking for somewhere to pupate. Balancing its pine needle home behind it, soon it will seal itself inside and emerge a few weeks later, ready to take to the air.

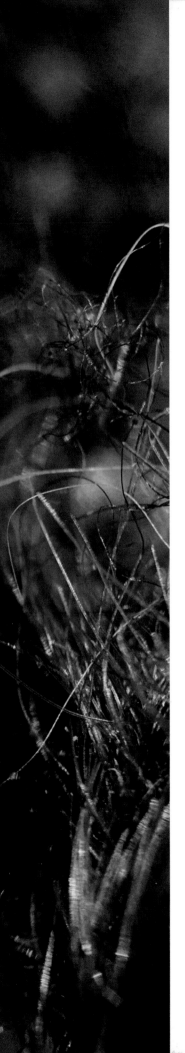

CONTENTS

OUT OF THE DARKNESS

How one thing leads to another

One of the most exciting aspects of natural history is the simple fact that, no matter how much you know, there are always new things to discover. One sunny spring morning I was out photographing orchids on the field by my house when I noticed a small hole in the earth. It was easily big enough to accommodate my thumb. Whilst probably no mystery to many, it was new to me. Too big for ants or worms, too small for mice or shrews – I really had no idea what had made such a neat burrow. Making a note of its position, I carried on with the orchids, keeping an eye out for more thumb-sized holes. I found three.

The following morning I got up early, set up my camera and sat down to watch the burrow nearest to the house, close enough to see but far enough away not to alarm whatever it may be. I waited all day – nothing. I knew I wasn't wasting my time as the burrows had to be fresh. The early spring had been so wet that any untended digging from last season would have collapsed. So the next day I did the same.

It was dusk when I saw the first stirrings. Peeking tentatively out of its burrow came a field cricket. In my excitement at patience rewarded I must have moved my head a millimetre and the cricket scurried back into the gloom – damn!

It took a week to get a decent shot. A virtually black creature in a tiny black hole is a photographic nightmare and it flatly refused to adopt a decent pose for me. Gradually though, it got used to being stared at all day and would settle for longer periods, sunning itself on its little veranda. Adult male field crickets sit at the entrance to their burrow and sing to attract a mate. It took a further two weeks for him to be successful and for me to photograph the happy couple.

And I told you all that to tell you this: whilst sitting motionless, staring at one small patch of grass for days on end, I was constantly enthralled by the huge variety of creatures that would pass my nose. The idea for this book was born from tiny holes and timid crickets.

Above and overleaf: Apart from size and genitalia, the primitive, ametabolous bristletails look the same throughout their lives.

Most entomologists would agree that if you are excited by new things, the insect world has more to offer than anything, with the possible exception of space exploration. To make a few comparisons, the world is home to around 5,000 different species of mammals. Goats to guinea pigs and dogs to dolphins, it is probably fair to say that few people would be surprised by the sight of newly discovered mammalian species. That is not to understate their beauty or wonder, simply that, in one way or another, they all seem familiar. Astonishingly, there are roughly 10,000 species of birds, twice as many as our own class, yet despite the extraordinary variation between tits, toucans, crows and cassowaries, they too, all seem comfortably familiar.

These seemingly vast numbers fall into perspective when we look at other classes. Reptiles and amphibians number somewhere in the region of 15,000 species, fish: approximately 26,000. Yet still these vast hordes become but a trifle when we delve into the world of the invertebrates, where the numbers climb relentlessly, even Pandora could not possess a box big enough.

A close up view of a bristletail, one of the world's most ancient orders.

Above: A dragonfly nymph searches for prey amidst the rocks and weeds of a stream bed.

There are around 60,000 different crustaceans, more than 75,000 species of arachnids; it seems unfathomable, yet even these numbers pale into insignificance when compared with insects. To date, science has named around a million, with estimates of the number of species remaining to be discovered being several million more. The most experienced entomologists in the world have only scratched the surface and exist happily in a world of constant learning and discovery.

Unsurprisingly, it would not have been possible to include every aspect of metamorphosis within the pages of a single book, so my intention here has been to illustrate some of the less well known, with others, that are more familiar but which hold hidden surprises. To that end, I have not dwelt on the ametabolous primitive orders such as the bristletails (Archaeognatha), which grow without visible changes, or the very well known, such as dragonflies, which have been photographed as many times as the cows have come home. That said, it is still a wonder that one of the insect world's strongest fliers begins life underwater.

SURVIVAL STRATEGIES

Coping with danger and competition

Imagine a world where nothing is ever still. Where every living moment is shaken and buffeted with all the ferocity of earthquakes and storms. It seems an unbearable thought, yet such is the world for the majority of surface-dwelling insects. At their minute scale, even the slightest breeze causes grass to whip, branches to shake and leaves to tremble. To the tiniest amongst them, the impact of a single raindrop can mean instant death. To some of the small burrowers and earth-dwelling larvae, the gently shimmering puddles after heavy rain may have been too great a deluge, condemning them to drown in cold, watery graves.

To make matters worse, there is the constant threat of predation from a substantial percentage of larger creatures, whether they be mammals, birds, fish or other insects. Even smaller creatures may be mites, ready to latch on and suck the haemolymph out of you, or parasites waiting for the opportunity to lay eggs inside defenceless bodies, or inside other eggs, or inside other parasites which are already inside other hosts …

Nowhere is safe – ever.

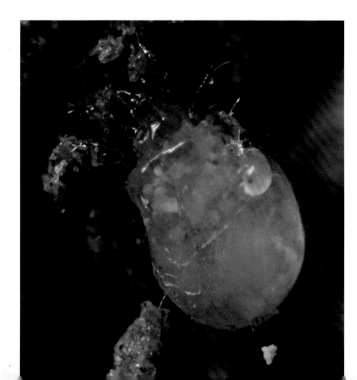

Opposite: A female *Orthetrum brunneum*. Dragonflies catch their prey in flight then settle to feed.

Left: Mites are everywhere waiting to latch on to a passing host. The larger individual is less than a millimetre in size and is carrying its own, even tinier unwanted guest.

Opposite: A Streak Moth caterpillar blending perfectly with its food plant.

Above: A newly hatched lacewing larva, looking almost demonic with its huge fang-like jaws. These formidable predators create a shield by piling the corpses of their prey onto their backs.

In the face of these dangers, evolution has given rise to some astonishing survival strategies for both self-preservation and ensuring the safety and success of offspring. Aside from the obvious tactic of producing as many young as possible, strategies range from cryptic camouflage to minimising competition for resources within the species. Developing a life cycle where larvae and adults not only live in different environments but depend upon completely different diets is a neat solution. Indeed, some species even evolve from diurnal larvae into nocturnal adults, thus ensuring that adult and offspring do not even occupy the same space.

So how does something as beautiful as a butterfly begin life as little more than a fancy maggot? Or something as elegant and delicate as a lacewing hatch out looking like a minuscule escapee from a horror movie? What are the circumstances which allow a creature to transform from one body

Blow fly larvae feeding on a rotting carcass. Abdominal segments bear a denticle belt, a ring of toothy protrusions which provide extra grip for ease of movement.

Be very grateful this page isn't scratch and sniff.

shape into another, often so utterly different from the first that you would be forgiven for thinking they were completely unrelated organisms? It is not always easy to make sense of the twists and turns of evolution, so whilst we have a sense of how and why some species developed these shape-shifting life cycles, the truth is, many allow us to do little more than accept that, in the natural world, sometimes things happen just because they can.

Imagine that your mother put you in a babygro that she never changed. You would, in a comparatively short period of time, stretch it to bursting point, exposing your delicate baby flesh to the risks of chafing and bruising. At this point your mother can't fail to notice your predicament and must provide you with a larger version. The cycle is repeated until babygros are either no longer a practical solution, or your changing life style demands something a little more sophisticated. The actual solution will depend on your individual circumstances, but let's suppose you now have a younger sibling vying for your mother's attention. Rather than fight this babygro-clad intrusion on your food supply and no longer constrained to do little more than wriggle, you find that your new dungarees with corduroy knee-pads give you a reasonable purchase on the tiled kitchen floor. Your escape from competition is assured as you crawl your way to the stash of Farley's Rusks in the kitchen cupboard.

For insects, of course, what allows this to happen is that marvel of evolution – the exoskeleton. Clearly there is no mother in attendance to change an insect's skin, but the analogy of clothes is not quite as silly as it sounds. For example, in place of 'babygro' and 'dungarees', read developing 'ventral denticle belt' (gloriously, also known as creeping welts) – spiny rings on the abdominal segments of fly larvae. As these belts develop the larvae can move much more easily through goo, to exploit fresh (I use the word loosely) food sources.

To pursue the analogy, we have the luxury of being able to change our chosen skin to suit our environmental needs and feeding habits. If we want to eat in the best restaurant we probably won't gain access to the food if we wear jeans and a t-shirt. Equally, if we want to climb a tree to eat an apple, we probably won't do it wearing the haute couture that got us into the restaurant. External changes are integral to a great many species, whether they be for feeding, camouflage, dispersal or attracting a mate. Essentially, evolution has provided insects with changes of skin, remarkably adapted to suit the demands of each stage within their myriad life cycles.

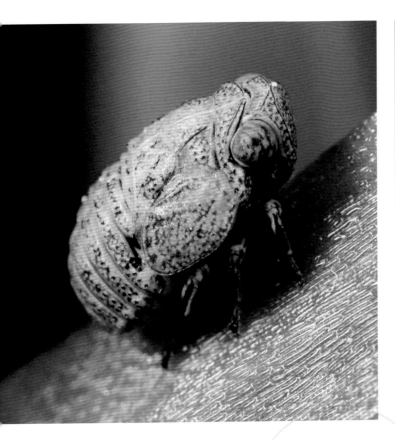

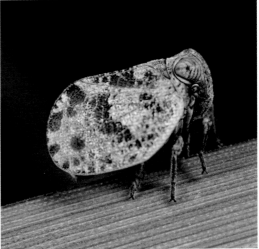

Left and above: Hemiptera are all hemimetabolous. Despite the noticeable difference between juvenile wing buds (left) and adult wings (above) the plant hopper *Hysteropterum dolichotum* is quite recognizable throughout its life cycle.

Opposite: By contrast, Hymenoptera are holometabolous. Here an ant carries a larva to safer territory. The difference between juvenile and adult forms could not be more stark.

METAMORPHOSIS

The process of change

The purpose of this book is to illustrate just a few of the countless shape-shifting aspects of insect life cycles that we might see in the wild, particularly if they reveal something unexpected or unfamiliar. Beneath the surface, the whole process of metamorphosis is an intricate balance of hormones, temperature, humidity, food and other influences, all engaged in a biochemical dance of such beautiful complexity that they demand a book of their own, not least of all because a photograph of any complex molecule will do little to help anyone in the field.

Consequently, the chemistry is presented here in an appropriately weevil-sized nutshell, more for the wonder of it all and to marvel at evolution's relentless ability to pull rabbits out of hats. Like children on a treasure hunt, our excited curiosity holds us, searching for the next clue in our quest

to understand how the trick was done. For those who know or wish to know their cercus from their trochanter, a selection of further reading can be found at the end of this book.

There are two distinct types of metamorphosis: hemimetabolous and holometabolous. Hemimetabolous (meaning incomplete metamorphosis) insects such as crickets, mantids and bugs, resemble the adult form throughout their lives. In these species the young are called nymphs and each moult brings them closer to their adult morphology. Conversely, the young of holometabolous (complete metamorphosis) insects, called larvae, look nothing like their adult form. These insects, which include butterflies, ants, beetles and flies, often resemble little more than hungry bags but transform into a breathtaking variety of body shapes and colours.

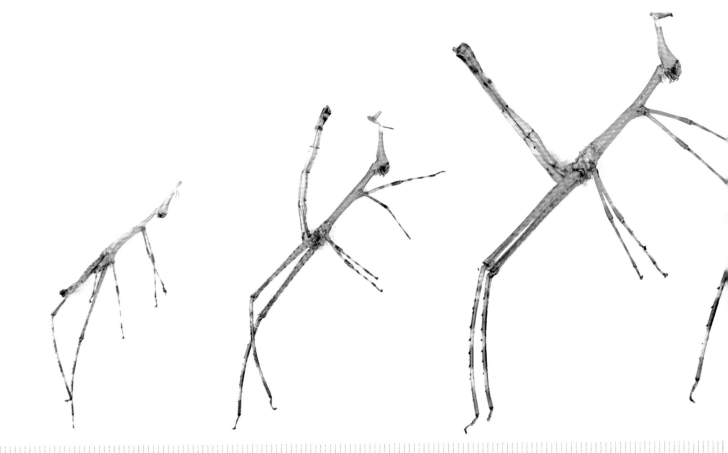

Prior to adulthood, each stage of development is called an instar, a newly hatched larva or nymph being its first. The first moult reveals the second instar and so on. In hemimetabolous insects, the final instar moults into the adult form. In holometabolous insects, the transition from larva to adult takes place in an intermediate stage called a pupa. Most species moult a handful of times before reaching adulthood, however the number of instars varies greatly between orders and species. Certain mayflies, for example, may moult more than 30 times, whilst primitive insects like springtails continue to moult throughout their lives.

Orthoptera, the grasshoppers and crickets, are fairly average in having five instars. Above, the moults of a single South American horsehead grasshopper show the growth

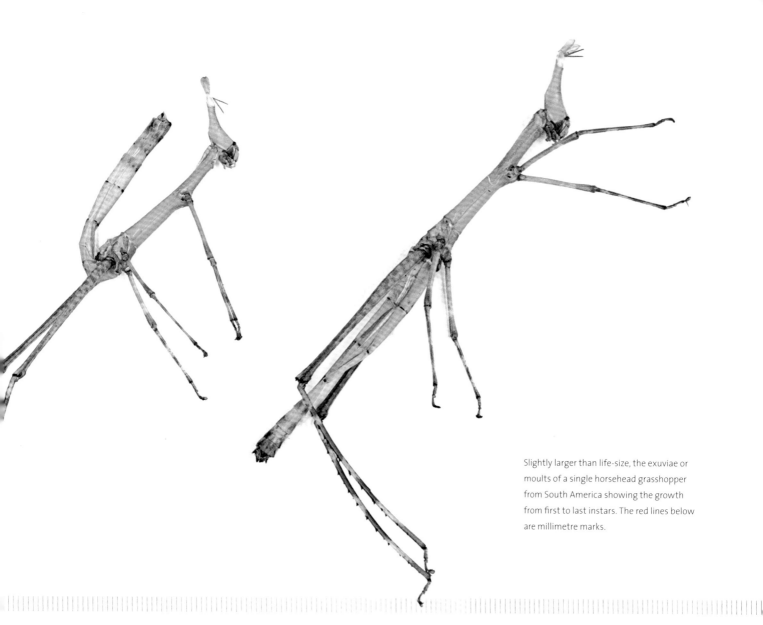

Slightly larger than life-size, the exuviae or moults of a single horsehead grasshopper from South America showing the growth from first to last instars. The red lines below are millimetre marks.

over approximately a 12-week period. Each stage lasts approximately three weeks so if the line were extended in both directions, the 18-week development would include a ten millimetre-long egg and a 16 centimetre long adult female, over half as long again as her fifth instar moult. We will return to these impressive hoppers later.

Common to all insects is the exoskeleton, a waterproof, protective outer wall, inside which the organs and soft tissues of the body are supported. But the specific characteristics of this outer shell differ widely. The fact that we call it an exo*skeleton* is, in itself, potentially misleading. Like the vertebrate skeleton it is a supporting structure, however it may or may not be completely rigid, thick or thin, and in some cases is very delicate indeed.

Above: A fresh-faced sawfly larva sheds its old skin. The dark, shed head capsule can be seen towards its rear end.

Below: Viewed from behind, the moult progresses and the flimsy exuvia is cast off like an old stocking.

For many larvae, particularly amongst holometabolous insects, the cuticle appears to be little more than a constraining bag which splits and falls away as it is outgrown by each successive instar. In the sawfly family for example, along with the majority of holometabolous larvae, this protective layer is a thin skin which can be shed relatively easily – an important factor as any insect is at its most vulnerable during these periods of change.

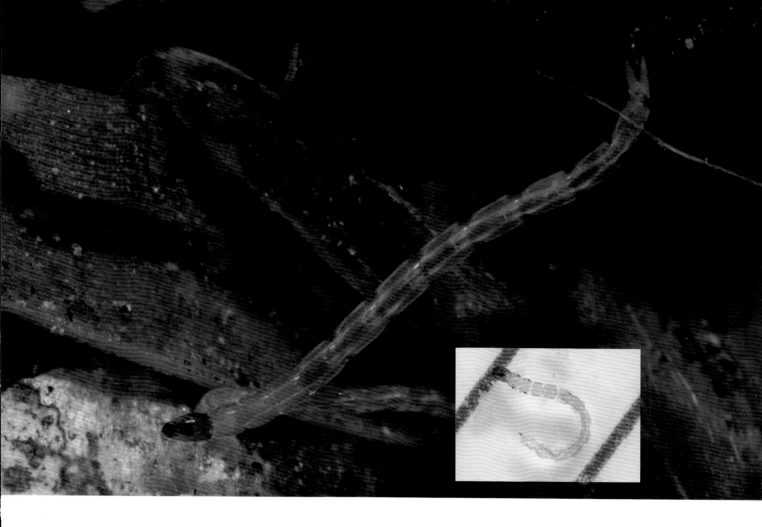

Above: The aquatic larvae of ceratopogonid midges. Inset: an early instar swims in a water droplet between the millimetre markings of a plastic ruler.

Below: These opportunist feeders may form a writhing mass as they fight to get at their food.

Despite this vulnerability, for some insects, moulting can be a long, drawn-out affair and none more so than the aquatic juveniles of biting midges (Ceratopogonidae). The larvae of these insects are highly active, sometimes seen as a tangled mass of individuals, trying to exploit the same food source.

They are consummate opportunists, grazing on algae or swooping in to feed on another larva's moult the very instant it has been shed.

Above: Illustrating the perils of moulting. At the pupal stage the juvenile midge becomes virually immobile, barely able to flick its tail. This pupa took almost a full day to free itself from the old skin.

It is not, however, the free-swimming larvae that face the greatest perils. It is their transition into the non-feeding pupa which is so fraught with danger. Exposed and helpless at the water surface, the larva's moult into pupal stage is dangerously slow. The individual above took almost a full day to shed its last larval skin, leaving it at the mercy of any number of potential predators.

Even when the moult is complete, the pupa remains virtually immobile, able only to move its tail rather feebly from side to side, so slowly that it barely seems deliberate. When sensing danger it can do no more than sink slowly out of harm's way and if it is lucky, the threat will have passed by the time it needs to return to the surface for air.

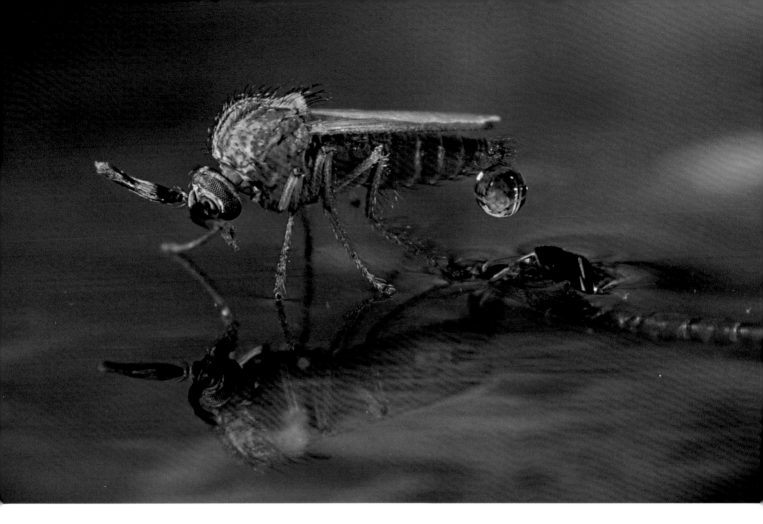

Fortunately this precarious phase is quite short and less than a week later the adult will climb out of the pupal skin, onto the water surface. The unrelenting numbers-game aspect of insect life is harshly illustrated by these semi-aquatic life cycles. If, through no more than bad luck, they pupate in windy weather, a gust may flatten their fragile drying bodies to the water surface. Once the water's surface tension is broken they will be lucky to drag themselves free.

Just as with us, the growth and development of insects is a complex, hormone-driven sequence of intricately balanced events. Nestling beside the insect brain are a pair of glands, the corpora allata, which, together with specialised cells within the brain itself, form the drivers for the metamorphic process. The glands secrete a juvenile hormone which suppresses the development of adult features, thereby constraining the larva or nymph to the purpose of growth. In the final instar, the corpora allata shrink away and hormone production is taken over by the specialist brain cells which secrete none of the adult-inhibiting chemistry. This hormonal shift allows the formation of the mature insect's characteristics such as reproductive organs and fully developed wings.

Hormonal balance is critical for all living organisms. We are familiar with wide-ranging problems when our own body chemistry becomes imbalanced, from diabetes to gigantism, headaches to acne, hormones rule our state of health. For insects, the negative potentials of hormone imbalance can be extreme.

Back in the 1930s, Vincent Wigglesworth, the foremost pioneer in our understanding of insect physiology, began performing experiments which revealed that if the brain or glands of different instars were removed and placed into others, specific development could be induced. Altering the hormone balance of an early larva to that of its final instar would result in a tiny adult at the next moult. Conversely, if a final instar's chemistry was forced to remain juvenile, instead of an adult being produced from the next moult, an even larger larva or nymph would appear.

The photograph opposite shows two caterpillars of *Attacus atlas*, the Giant Atlas Moth from south-east Asia. At first glance they appear to be at different stages of development but actually, both individuals hatched on the same day from eggs laid by the same female. Both are in their final instar, the only difference being a hormonal imbalance preventing one from growing. Only the larger one has gained enough fat reserves to survive the four-week period pupating inside a cocoon. Perhaps more surprising, is that long after its giant sibling has drifted into silk-bound slumbers, our tiny runt just continues eating. Weeks pass, gradually feeding slows and eventually stops. Finally it dies, in this case, around the same time as the healthy sibling emerged from its cocoon in full winged splendour.

The insect world is filled with surprises, many beautiful, others horrific. Either way, a closer look can only increase immeasurably our sense of wonder at the extraordinary intricacies of their lives.

Two *Attacus atlas* larvae, exactly the same age, illustrate how a hormone imbalance can dramatically affect an insect's development, in this case, fatally preventing growth.

ORTHOPTERA

Grasshoppers, crickets and their relatives

From solitary earth-dwellers to swarming airborne pests, the 20,000 or so species of orthopterans are most commonly recognised by their long back legs and accompanying hopping ability. Despite appearances however, the hop itself may or may not be particularly useful. Some grasshoppers will make a powerful leap into the air, spreading their wings as they do so and flying some considerable distance. By contrast, field crickets (below) make better use of their legs for digging burrows, and exhibit a singularly unimpressive hop which looks more like a panic response than a bold predator-evasive tactic.

These hemimetabolous insects typically pass through five instars, although in some species it can be as many as nine. From a somewhat questionable level of objectivity, orthopteran nymphs do score highly on the entomologist's scale of cuteness.

Opposite: Just a few millimetres long, a first-instar bush cricket climbs across the crystal-textured surface of a Lady orchid, *Orchis purpurea*.

Above: Even in the early instars, the armour-like orthopteran pronotum is already pronounced.

Left: A final-instar field cricket emerges from hibernation and repairs the burrow in preparation for his final moult. Then he will be able to sing to attract a mate.

The order comprises two suborders which, for a change, are satisfyingly simple to distinguish. Ensifera, the crickets and katydids, are most clearly recognised by their long, tapering antennae. Sometimes, particularly in early-instar nymphs (above), the antennae are so disproportionately long that it seems miraculous that the insects manage to find any balance at all.

Ensiferan females have prominent ovipositors and mating often involves nuptial gifts. Males produce a spermatophore which, as well as the sperm, contains a gelatinous feast. The mated female (right) is in the process of eating her nutritious prize.

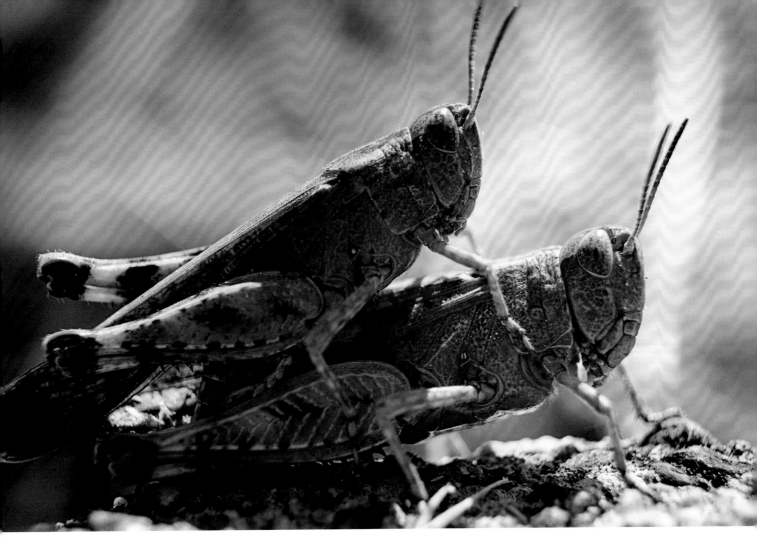

Above: The majority of caeliferans have long powerful wings, as seen in this mating pair of Field Grasshoppers, *Chorthippus brunneus*.

Below: The wing buds of immature orthopterans may have ridges, but no distinct venation.

Ensiferan singing, or stridulation, is performed by the forewings being rubbed together. By contrast, the second suborder, the Caelifera, which includes all the grasshoppers, bush hoppers and locusts, generally produce their song by rubbing hind legs against forewings.

Caelifera are sun-loving vegetarians with much shorter antennae, making them easy to distinguish from ensiferans. Most species are strong fliers, although some are wingless and others are brachypterous, meaning short-winged, often reduced to little more than flaps. If only

Above: A mating pair of brachypterous *Pezotettix giornae*. Despite the tiny wings, their maturity is evident.

Below: The venation is clearly visible on the adult *Pezotettix* wing.

glimpsed briefly, these stubby-winged species can easily be mistaken for juveniles with undeveloped wing buds. The tell-tale difference is that mature wings have clear venation which the immature, developing wings of any species do not (opposite below). The photographs above show two mating pairs (so clearly adults) of very similar-looking grasshoppers. On the left, the fully winged Common Field Grasshopper, *Chorthippus brunneus*, on the right, the brachypterous *Pezotettix giornae*. Despite the tiny size of the latter's wings, the venation can clearly be seen.

As hatching approaches, the House Cricket nymph is just visible through the shell of the two millimetre-long egg.

Despite the name, House Crickets, *Acheta domesticus*, are widespread in any suitably warm environment. They do not hibernate and can become a pest if they take up residence in predator-free domestic places such as bakeries. With a life cycle of two to three months, they can continue to breed all year round and increase in numbers quite rapidly.

Outdoors, the two millimetre-long eggs are laid in moist soil and usually take around two weeks to hatch. Cricket eggs remain quite opaque but as hatching approaches, the nymph's dark eyes and abdominal segments gradually become more visible. The tiny first-instar nymphs are highly active as soon as they hatch and begin to explore their surroundings within minutes of leaving the egg. Although pale and almost transparent at first, their appearance darkens over the following day or two but they remain well camouflaged and soil-like in colour.

A newly hatched nymph stands beside its empty egg. The round hole and ragged tear through which it emerged can be seen at the left-hand end of the egg.

The gregarious nymphs develop quite quickly, passing through up to nine instars in six or seven weeks. Although there is a noticeable difference between first and last instars, the successive changes are extremely subtle and sometimes impossible to see.

As they mature, the later instars and adults can become fairly aggressive fighters with disputes over territory. Battle scars and lost limbs are not unusual.

Above: Close to the final moult, movement becomes all but impossible.

Below: Having lost a hind leg in a fight, this final instar's swollen abdomen is clear to see.

They are also very unfussy eaters, often consuming their own or each other's exuviae. Cannibalism is another common behaviour, although this is more a case of taking advantage of the valuable nutrients of a dead body, than actually killing each other for food.

Moults appear to be exhausting and none more so than the last. Their bodies grow increasingly distended, something much easier to see in the photograph left, where the unfortunate

Above and below: Dragging itself slowly from the old skin, the wings hang like crumpled fabric.

individual's missing hind leg reveals its swollen abdomen. A period of immobility follows as the old and new skins separate. The old exoskeleton then splits down the mid-line of head and thorax, giving the emerging adult the freedom to crawl slowly forwards.

Fully shedding the old exoskeleton will take an hour or two, and the effort seems to be so great that sometimes a cricket gives the impression that it is just going to give up halfway through. Even

Above: Finally free from the old skin, this adult male will rest to allow its new exoskeleton to dry and harden.

Right: Forewings raised in confident singing pose. The song is created by rubbing the scraper of one wing against the stridulatory file of the other.

before they are pumped into shape, it seems impossible that the new, full-sized wings ever fitted inside the old exoskeleton. Finally though, having heaved itself free, the exhausted adult will rest to allow its pale, ghostly form to dry and harden.

A couple of days later, although it takes a little practice to reach full volume, the adult male is already beginning to sing. The main photograph shows how the forewings are raised to rub the scraper of the underlying wing against the file on the underside of the top wing.

A mating pair of Peruvian Horsehead Grasshoppers, the smaller green male is on the female's back. An endearing feature of the species is their eternally surprised expression.

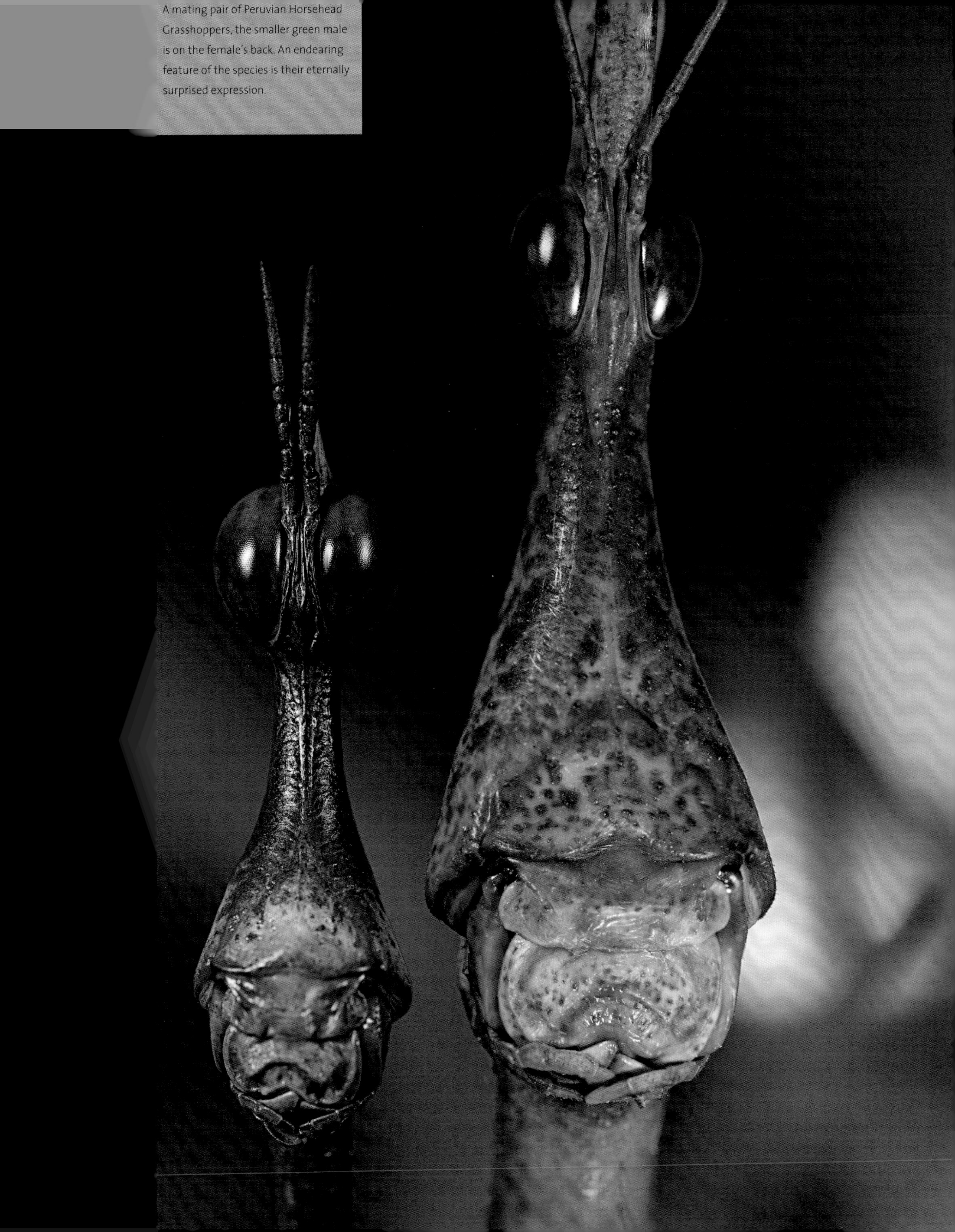

There could hardly be a greater contrast with the full-winged singing crickets than the wingless and very silent Horsehead Grasshoppers (*Pseudoproscopia latirostris*) from Peru. These extraordinary creatures (apart from scoring maximum points on the previously mentioned scale of cuteness) are much more like (and often mistaken for) stick insects than grasshoppers in their behaviour. With their extremely long back legs they are more than capable of jumping, but prefer to mooch casually about in the canopy than hop around in the grass.

Above: A female Peruvian Horsehead Grasshopper. This species is much more at home amongst the branches than on the ground.

Unlike House Crickets, whose sexes look very similar (apart from the female's obvious ovipositor), sexual dimorphism is highly conspicuous in the horseheads. The slender, dark green males are much smaller than the heavy, mottled brown females, usually reaching lengths of around 10cm against the female's 16cm.

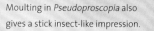

Moulting in *Pseudoproscopia* also gives a stick insect-like impression.

Above: Male Peruvian Horsehead Grasshoppers are distinctly slimmer than the larger females.

Below: A female buries her abdomen as deeply as she can when ovipositing.

The moulting behaviour of the species is also more akin to phasmids than other orthopterans, as the nymphs suspend themselves from leaves and branches in precisely the same way. It typically takes around 12 weeks to pass through the five instars from hatching to adulthood (see page 22) and the adults tend to live for around another seven months.

One aspect of behaviour that is distinctly unlike that of phasmids however, is that rather than simply dropping or flicking their eggs to the ground, females will bury their abdomens as deeply as possible into a moist substrate to lay their eggs out of harm's way.

PHASMATODEA

The stick and leaf insects

Throughout the entire natural world, the 2,500 or so species of leaf and stick insects are unmatched in their camouflage. Even their eggs resemble plant seeds and, in some species, are often carried off by ants, which take them back to their nests where they remain in safety until the nymphs emerge. The tiny first instars then make their way to the surface and climb the nearest vegetation to begin their life in the foliage.

Probably the best plant-mimics are the 50 or so species of leaf insects, the Phylliidae, from south east Asia and Australasia. When disturbed, they rock gently back and forth, reinforcing the deception by appearing to be leaves swaying in the breeze. Wing buds begin to appear in the tiny second-instar nymphs (left) and ultimately, become so leaflike as to render the adults all but invisible amongst the leaves.

Above: Eggs of the leaf insect *Phyllium philippinicum* look just like plant seeds.

Opposite: Just 22mm long, a second-instar leaf insect is just developing its wing buds.

Left: By the final instar the wing buds are clearly visible, but still very small in comparison with the adult.

Overleaf: An adult female *Phyllium phillipinicum*. Despite the impressive wings, the females are flightless.

Opposite and above: A European stick insect, *Clonopsis gallica*, emerging from its 2mm-long egg. The small disc to the right in the main paicture is the egg's covering lid, called an operculum, which the nymph pops off as it begins to emerge.

The stick insects, Phasmatidae, whilst more commonly found in tropical regions, are much more widespread than their leafy cousins. They come in all manner of shapes and sizes, and include the world's largest insect, *Phobaeticus chani* from Borneo, which measures almost half a metre in length. The fact that such a huge insect was only discovered in the first decade of the 21st century is a clear testimony to these creatures' amazing camouflage.

The eggs of mated females may produce nymphs of either sex. However, parthenogenesis (asexual reproduction) is common throughout the order and will almost always produce solely female offspring. Their start in life is so improbably vulnerable that it is almost a miracle of nature that any of them survive at all. The European species, *Clonopsis gallica* shown here, emerges from a 2mm long egg in a helpless tangle of stringy legs. Occasionally, if the nymph is lucky,

Above: Although hatching may be fairly quick in ideal conditions, some nymphs can drag themselves around for hours before all their legs are free.

Below: The crumpled legs are almost useless for some hours, before sufficient fluids are pumped through to bring rigidity.

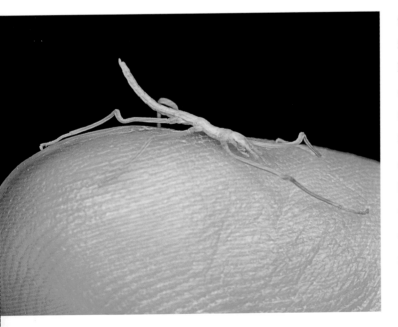

the hatching process can be fairly quick, but often it is an exhausting struggle to wrestle so gangly a body from so confined a space. A frequent occurrence is that the hatchling will manage to free two or three legs and then spend hours heaving itself around until the egg snags on something which it can then pull against. Even worse, sometimes the legs are so badly tangled and knotted inside the egg that the nymph cannot break free at all and will simply die from its struggles.

Once the tiny, 10mm long nymph has successfully pulled itself from the egg, its fragile

Above: A second-instar nymph in characteristic pose.

Below: First-instar nymphs have noticeably flatter abdomens which become more rounded after the first moult.

body is inflated with air and fluids, a process which may take up to a few hours. Then, with functioning legs at last, it will climb up into the leaves to take on the tasks of eating and pretending to be a stick.

Most phasmids pass through five or six instars and the moults usually take place every three to four weeks. In the wingless species, apart from growing larger, there are few discernable changes before sexual maturity. The only significant difference is that unlike older juveniles, the abdomens of first-instar nymphs are fairly flattened (right).

For stick insects, moulting appears to be every bit as strenuous as hatching. A couple of days before each moult, nymphs will stop eating and become very sluggish. Very often they will find a comfortable spot and stop moving altogether until ready to cast off the old skin.

Clonopsis gallica typically moult in the early morning, usually just before sunrise. Clinging on by their back legs, they hang downwards to get as much assistance as possible from gravity. As with nearly all insects, levels of humidity make an enormous difference to the length of time it takes to fully emerge from each moult. The individual opposite took a little over two hours to separate itself fully, find a suitable position to dry off and allow the new exoskeleton to harden.

Opposite and above: The moult itself may take an hour or two and after a short drying-off period, enthusiastic eating is resumed.

One of the notable survival tactics of stick insects is their ability to shed limbs in order to escape predation. The discarded leg will normally be regrown at the subsequent moult, although this becomes less reliable as the nymphs mature. Adults will also sacrifice legs if necessary, but these will not regenerate.

One quite strange feature of limb regeneration in stick insects is a process called antennapedia, meaning 'antennal feet'. Due to the similarity of genes between limbs and antennae, a shed antenna may regrow as a leg.

Another interesting characteristic of the seed-like eggs of stick insects, is an example of something happening in nature just because it can, rather than it holding any significant evolutionary advantage. In the photographs above, the two-millimetre long eggs of the European *Clonopsis gallica* are shown beside the five-millimetre long eggs of the Australasian species *Extatosoma tiaratum*.

In the photograph above right, the top two rows were randomly selected from many hundreds of eggs laid by about 20 individuals. Apart from slight differences in shade, the eggs are identical. The bottom two rows, also chosen at random from roughly 100 eggs, show 10, all laid by a single unmated female. The 10 may as well have been 50, or 100. The point is that they are all quite different. Whilst there is always a degree of variability, the eggs of individual phasmid species tend to be quite distinctive. It is impossible to say with any certainty why species such as *Extatosoma tiaratum* evolved such an inconsistent

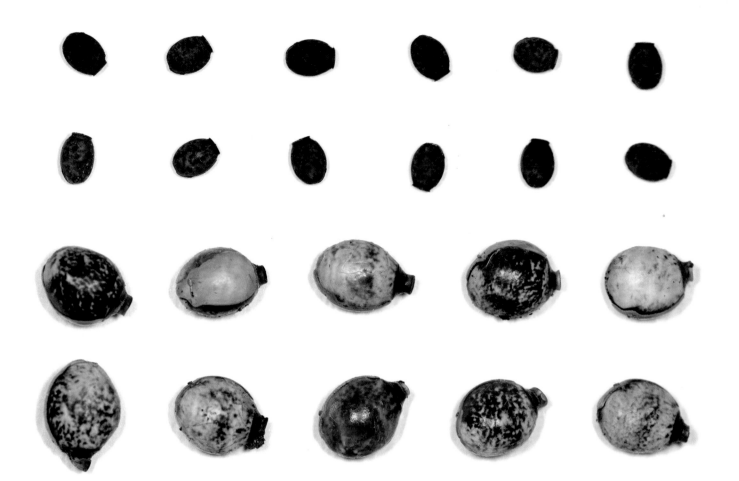

egg pattern. Perhaps such changeability ensures that at least one or two will be better camouflaged against the ground, or maybe, with the difference in heat absorption, the lights and darks create variations in gestation periods, preventing the young from emerging together and thereby reducing competition.

More remarkable still is that despite the progeny from an unmated female being genetically identical, the resulting offspring may be as varied in colour as the eggs from which they emerged.

Opposite: An egg of the European *Clonopsis gallica* beside that of the much larger Australasian *Extatosoma tiaratum*.

Above: A comparison between the consistently identical eggs of *Clonopsis gallica* with the extremely variable colouration of *Extatosoma tiaratum*.

Opposite: A hatching *Extatosoma tiaratum* nymph struggles to break free from its egg.

Above: The second-instar nymphs have a dramatically different morphology and curl their abdomens in mimicry of a scorpion when alarmed.

Eggs of all Phasmatodea take a long time to hatch. It is no great surprise that eggs of species in cooler climates, when laid in late summer, will overwinter and not hatch until the spring. Slightly more of a surprise however, is that even in tropical regions where temperature is fairly constant throughout the year, eggs will still lie dormant for long periods and commonly take between six and nine months to hatch.

It is quite remarkable how the nymphs of any species of stick insect can develop to their full hatching size within the confines of such tiny eggs. It is even more astonishing with the first instar nymphs of *Extatosoma tiaratum* from Australasia (left) and it seems impossible that they can remain inside for so long without the egg bursting open under the pressure of the developing nymph.

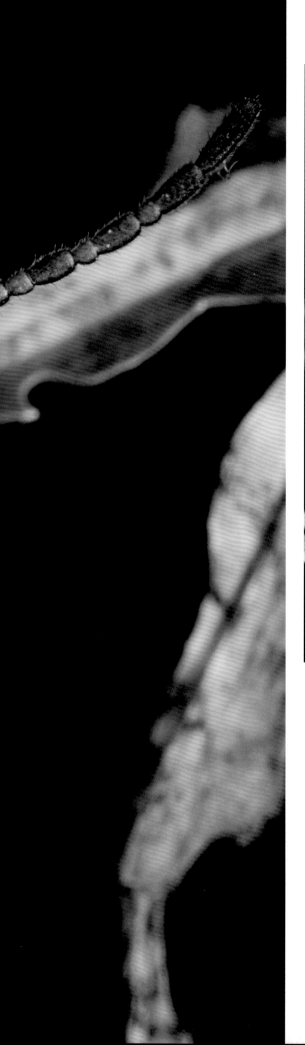

The anatomy of mouthparts is complex in most insects but the intricate arrangement is much easier to see in stick insects, largely due to their tendency to behave like sticks and stay still for longer. The most notable features are the finger-like palps and blade-like mandibles. The sensory palps are almost like pairs of hands clasped to the chin, which stabilise the leaf whilst it is cut away by the mandibles.

As they develop, their spiny protrusions become more pronounced and, if provoked, they can give an impressive pinch by folding a limb on the potential predator. Although completely harmless, the spines can dig in painfully enough to startle the threat away.

Overall lifespans of *Extatosoma tiaratum* can range from four to six months as nymphs, followed by a further six to nine months as adults. In the photograph opposite, a third-instar nymph has begun seeking a convenient spot for its next moult. Once satisfied, it will remain motionless for anything up to a few days while the new exoskeleton gradually separates from the old outer

Opposite: A nymph may spend many hours finding a suitable place to moult.

Above: Pumping air through the body helps the emerging nymph to separate from its old skin.

Opposite and above: Heaving itself from the old skin, the nymph pulls downwards until just the tip of the abdomen remains attached. Safely back on a leaf, the nymph eats the shed skin as its first meal.

Above: The adult female is a far bulkier creature than in all its previous instars and can grow up to 15cm in length.

skin. Hanging by its back legs, the nymph pulls downwards until just the tip of the abdomen remains attached. Then, with the freed front legs, it will pull itself back upwards to allow the final tissues to separate. How long the fresh-faced nymph will need to rest for the new skin to dry varies a great deal and may be anything from 30 minutes to a few hours. Time of day probably has a bearing on this as, although stick insects are much more active at night (with less risk of predation), there doesn't seem to be a preference for nocturnal moulting.

Right: The tiny wings of adult female *Extatosoma tiaratum* are completely non-functional.

The cast-off skin is commonly, but not always, the first meal after a moult. It is difficult to say why this feeding habit is so unpredictable but certainly, if the exuvia drops to the ground it will be completely ignored.

In all species of leaf and stick insects, the females usually undergo one more moult than the males, most commonly five in males and six in females. Sexual dimorphism across the order is hugely variable with the sexes of some species (like *Clonopsis gallica* which we looked at earlier) being difficult to tell apart, other than from length of antennae.

Others, however, display huge differences and in *Extatosoma tiaratum* the females of the species (on these pages) are significantly larger than the males, which are slender, long-winged, strong-flying creatures. By contrast, the adult females are amongst the heaviest of insects, and have a reduced pair of wings which are completely non-functional.

MANTODEA

The mantises

Mantises must surely be the aliens in our midst. Their ability to turn their heads and stare us straight in the eye makes them appear far more intelligent than other insects, and of the world's 2,000 species, many display some remarkable behaviour. They are often cryptically camouflaged and it is sometimes easier to spot the movement of an obviously dead insect, than the outline of the mantis responsible for moving it around. The raptorial front legs are a complex combination of spines which simultaneously grip and impale their prey.

Another impressive characteristic is their ability to remain utterly motionless for long periods and then react with such speed that they can pluck flying insects from the air. Hunting success clearly increases with practice and experience. On many occasions I have watched juveniles make repeated unsuccessful strikes, whilst an adult is more likely to wait for the prey to be perfectly positioned before launching a single deadly attack.

Above: The swirling patterns in the eye of a third instar *Empusa pennata* contrast greatly with the plainer *Mantis religiosa*.

Left: The intricate arrangement of spines on the foreleg of a *Mantis religiosa*.

Opposite: Mantises have acute binocular vision and can judge the distance to prey with extreme accuracy.

Above: *Mantis religiosa* nymphs emerge from their papery egg case, called an ootheca.

Below: A cross section showing how the ootheca is layered, giving each egg its own compartment.

Mantis eggs are laid in a frothy mass called an ootheca. The female secretes a liquid which she whips into a foam with her hind legs, adding layer after layer lengthways rather like a puff pastry. The eggs are deposited evenly within the layers of foam which then hardens into a protective case. Watching them hatch, they just seem to emerge through the surface and it is difficult to see how they actually exit the ootheca. A cross-section of a spent egg case reveals how the nymphs break free of the eggs and then work their way upwards to push themselves out between the 'leaves'. The nymphs undergo their first moult very soon after hatching and it is only from the second instar that they begin to hunt for prey.

Less than a minute old, a *Mantis religiosa* nymph climbs away from its egg case and sees sunlight for the first time.

Above: A final instar female of the brown form of *Mantis religiosa*.

Distinguishing males from females is not always easy, however, the visible differences between the sexes can be seen above. *Mantis religiosa*, the most abundant of the European species is found in green or brown forms. Here, the brown female above has noticeably shorter antennae than the green male on the right. In some species, as well as being longer, the males' antennae can be bushy or feathered. The other key difference, which is only visible from around the fourth instar onwards, is that the males have one more abdominal segment than the females.

Mantises usually pass through 10 to 12 instars although in some species the number can be far fewer. Wing buds begin to appear quite early but are not particularly distinct until the nymphs are fairly developed. The two individuals above are both in their final instars.

Above: A final instar male of the green form of *Mantis religiosa*. Note the longer antennae and abdomen than the female opposite.

Below: The prominent eye-spot inside the foreleg is used in threat displays.

Photographed enjoying the remains of what was a rather large horse fly, the individual on the right shows another characteristic feature of *Mantis religiosa*. The inside of the forelegs bear prominent eye-spots which are sometimes used as a threat or warning display. These may be plain black, or black with a central white spot, as seen here.

Above and opposite: The final moult takes an hour or so, and as long again to pump the wings to their full glory. Unusually, this individual moved to another plant as soon as it was free of the old skin.

As the final moult approaches, feeding stops and the mantis looks for a safe and suitable place to prepare itself. Once satisfied, it will remain motionless for as long as a couple of days before suspending itself, upside down, very much like a stick insect. The skin splits at the thorax and the pale adult drops out of the old skin until just the hind legs are still holding on. Then, pulling itself upright, it holds fast with its forelegs and allows the hind legs to drop free. Once free of the old exoskeleton, the crumpled wings will be pumped to their full size, a task that may take an hour or two.

One feature common to all mantis nymphs, to a lesser or greater extent, is that the abdomen is always curved upwards behind them like a tail. One species in which this is particularly prominent is *Empusa pennata* (Empusidae) shown here.

Empusidae have very long prothoracic segments so as the wing buds begin to grow, they appear to be remarkably low on the body, protected by the upturned abdomen.

Above and opposite: *Empusa pennata*, like its cousin *Mantis religiosa*, may be green or brown. These early instars show the characteristically upturned abdomen of all mantis nymphs.

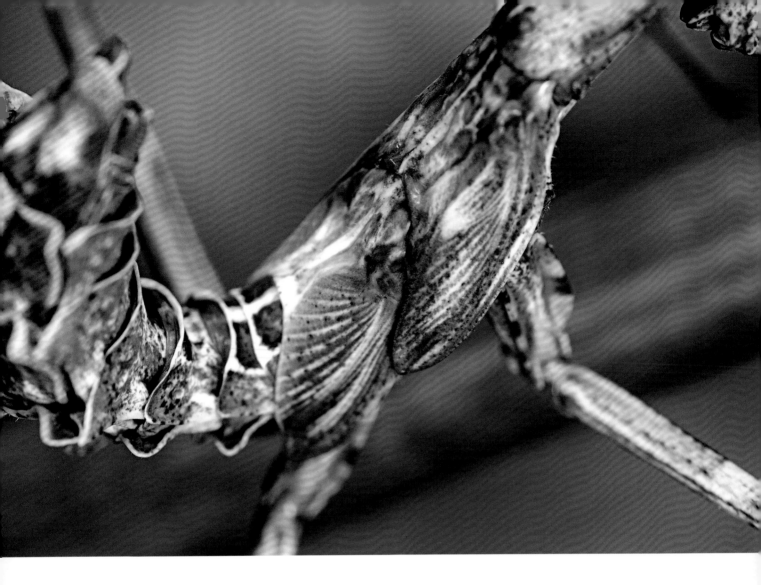

Above: As the nymph matures, the abdomen begins to straighten, offering a clearer view of the developing wing buds.

Opposite: The adult wings extend beyond the abdomen as can be seen in this mature female *Empusa pennata* of the green form.

Overleaf: A closer look at the crown-jewel-like crest and ocelli of both sexes. Ocelli of the male are red.

In later instars, the wing buds become noticeably more prominent and the abdomen becomes progressively straighter. At adulthood, the curve is lost completely and the fully developed wings extend beyond the tip of the abdomen.

Although many mantises are cannibalistic during mating, female Empusidae never eat their mates. Perhaps their finest feature is the raised crest which looks as if it could have inspired the dramatic headdresses of the Egyptian pharaohs. The crest is shorter in the males, an aspect for which they more than compensate with their enormously long feathery antennae and ruby-like ocelli. In females the ocelli are clear and more glass-like, but the impression given by both sexes is that they are wearing the crown jewels of the insect world.

PSOCOPTERA

Bark and book lice

Ranging in size from around 0.5mm to 10mm, the majority of Psocoptera are a test for the human eye. They are hemimetabolous, the juveniles resembling the adults and, as if identifying minuscule creatures isn't hard enough, many of the 3,000 or so species are wingless. This makes it even more difficult for the unititiated to tell the difference between a very tiny adult, or the nymph of something slightly larger.

In most species, psocoptera nymphs generally pass through five or six instars before reaching the adult stage in approximately two months. Once adulthood is reached they may live for around six months. In some of the winged families, wing buds can begin to appear as early as the second instar. In wingless forms however, the changes between instars are extremely subtle and mostly likely, only visible through a microscope if at all.

Above: As *Graphopsocus* nymphs mature the wing buds become very distinct, but remain very hard to spot. This individual is just a couple of millimetres long.

Left: *Graphopsocus cruciatus*, a winged species of barklouse. showing the characteristic psocopteran bulbous forehead. At 4mm in length, this is one of the medium-sized species

Reproduction amongst psocopterans is varied. A small number of species give birth to live young and parthenogenesis is common across the order. A useful detail which can help to narrow down identification is that winged psocoptera bear three primitive, light-sensing organs called ocelli (left), whereas wingless forms, such as the Liposcelidae above, have none. So an apparently wingless individual with ocelli will be a nymph of a winged species. Without ocelli, it may be a wingless adult.

Although many species are solitary, some, like the liposcelid book lice, are particularly gregarious. For creatures so small, the social species display some remarkably complex

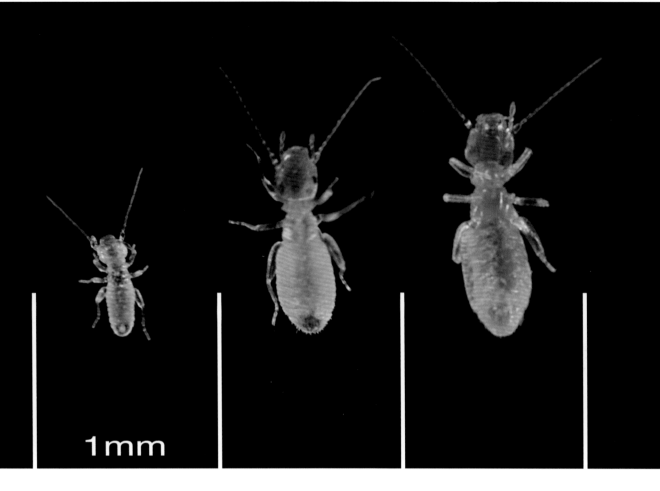

1mm

behaviour including a variety of courtship rituals. They can also communicate with sounds generated by a form of stridulation using specialised organs in the hind legs.

My own first experience of these creatures was whilst tidying up specimen containers in my studio. At first, I thought I had imagined it when a speck of dust moved. Then I thought it was my breath, until I noticed another one moving in the opposite direction. Closer inspection showed them to be liposcelidid book lice, a pest in museums or archives of paper materials. Despite the name, most species are at home in moist environments and more likely to be found in leaf litter.

Opposite: Just 1mm in length, a *Liposcelis terricolis* peers over the edge of a single sheet of paper.

Above: Rotated to face the same direction for the purpose of comparison. These three individuals were in a small plastic container, grazing together on compost.

HEMIPTERA

The true bugs

S hield bugs, cicadas, water boatmen, aphids, leaf hoppers – these are just a small selection of arguably the most morphologically varied of all the insect orders. But leaving aside shape, size and diet, the defining feature of all 82,000 known species of Hemiptera is a piercing beak, called a rostrum, through which they suck the juices from plant or prey.

Most bugs are herbivorous, all predatory species being within the suborder Heteroptera where the rostrum is positioned at the front of the head, making it much more mobile. The rostrum itself varies significantly across the order, clearly illustrated by comparing the long, three-segmented beak of the assassin bug on the left, with the short, four-segmented version of the backswimmer or water boatman below.

Above: With well over 2,000 species, aphids are significant plant pests throughout the world.

Left: Almost glass-like in its transparency, a first-instar *Notonecta maculata* nymph shows its short, broad rostrum.

Opposite: An assassin bug, *Rhinocoris iracundus* (Reduviidae) feasts on an earwig, sucking the juices through its piercing rostrum – the defining feature of all the true bugs.

Above: Just 2mm long, a first instar backswimmer (*Notonecta maculata*) floats upside-down, just below the water surface.

Right: A week later, it has moulted and the second-instar nymph is already 3mm in length.

The tiny first-instar nymphs of backswimmers or water boatmen (Notonectidae) measure about 2mm in length but are voracious feeders nonetheless, subduing almost anything small enough for them to grasp in their powerful front legs. They use the rostrum to stab their prey, injecting toxic saliva which also helps to break down tissues, making the resulting soup easier to digest.

There are five nymphal instars and development from hatching to adulthood takes around two months, depending on temperature and abundance of food. To the naked eye the nymph doesn't look like much, but in a matter of days it has increased in size by 50 per cent and after the first moult, the glasslike transparency takes on a more pearlescent appearance. Seen from below, against the sky, this makes them

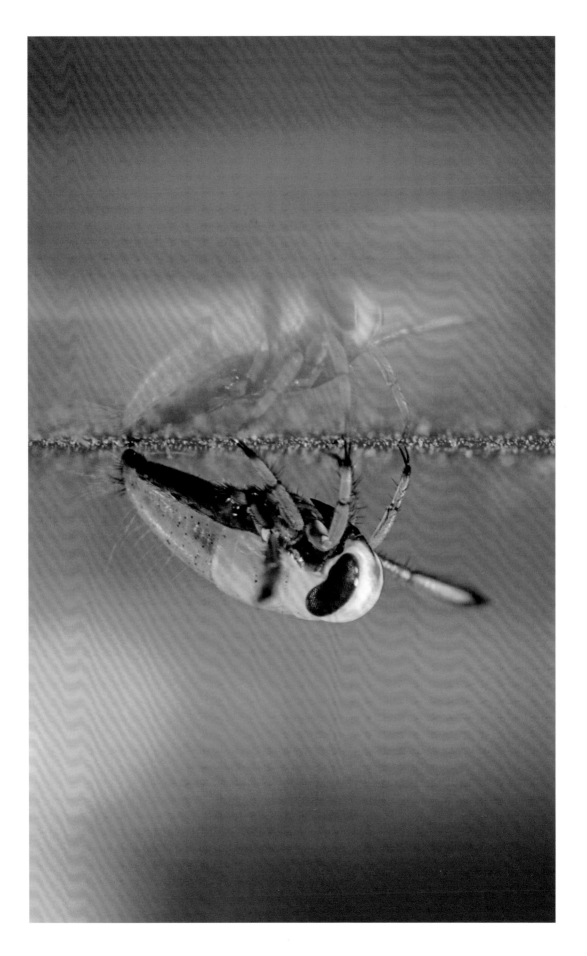

virtually invisible to predators. Notonectidae prey most commonly consists of species such as midge and mosquito larvae, but as they grow they will take on progressively larger victims including tadpoles and even small fish. They are however, particularly unfussy eaters and will just as readily resort to cannibalism if another nymph is careless enough to get too close.

Wing buds begin to appear by the third instar but are only clearly noticeable from the fourth. The final moult normally takes place between seven and eight weeks after hatching and in *Notonecta maculata* the transformation is striking, with the almost colourless nymph

becoming a richly coloured orange and black adult. On warm days the strong and noisy fliers will take to the air in search of new ponds and lakes, although it is difficult to say what prompts this behaviour. In my own research with specimens kept separately in identical environments and with exactly the same food, their eagerness to take flight after reaching adulthood has ranged from one week, to an individual that took a full three months. The more leisurely one only flew off when pushed to do so; convinced that it must have been either injured or ill, I took it out of the water to check, whereupon it promptly flew away.

Opposite: A second-instar nymph feeds on a midge pupa.

Above: Happy to eat anything, a third-instar nymph has caught a younger sibling.

Right: An adult *Notonecta maculata*. Backswimmers will often cling to submerged rocks and plants to save energy in moving water or in bad weather.

Above left: A cluster of *Piezodorus literatus* eggs with millimetre markings for scale.

Above: The first-instar nymphs develop their colouring within an hour or so of hatching.

Left: Moulting less than a week later, the markings of a second-instar nymph have changed very little.

Opposite: From the third-instar onwards, pale green becomes the dominant colouration.

A third instar nymph, still with dark pronotum, seems to shelter itself behind a fourth-instar older sibling which has now developed wing buds and a more uniform colour.

The time between moults can be less than two weeks, this pair clearly illustrating how rapidly nymphs can grow in ideal conditions.

Of all the Hemiptera, the Pentatomidae family or shield bugs can be truly confusing when it comes to recognising nymphal stages of different species. In some cases, if all five instars and adult form of a single shield bug were seen side by side, to the casual observer, they would almost certainly appear to be at least three different species.

Nymphs of the Gorse Shieldbug (*Piezodorus literatus*) are bright orange when they emerge from the egg, but within a couple of hours have developed their striking black, orange and white markings. The first moult happens after around four days and apart from being bigger and a little more streamlined, the second-instar nymphs are easily recognised as the same species. Two weeks later however, the emerging third-instar nymph begins to change. The black pronotum becomes patchy, the orange and black abdominal markings become more refined and the white ground has become a speckled pale green. After some rapid growth and another moult, the fourth instar has almost completely lost its black pigmentation. The pronotum now matches the abdomen and all appendages have turned yellow and orange.

After the next moult, the coloration of fifth-instar nymphs begins to darken again and the wing buds have extended over the abdomen. By contrast, the legs have lost most of their colour.

Two weeks later and the see-sawing changes continue. Having become paler in the fourth instar, with the exception of its legs, the nymph begins to darken again in its fifth. The wing buds are now much darker, particularly the areas corresponding with the corium and cuneus, the two outer sections of the adult's forewings. The paler triangular section between the wingbuds, known as the scutellum, is lighter but not as pale as the abdomen, which is now as vibrant a green as it will ever be. The last vestiges of the early instars' orange and black markings, which have become progressively smaller with each moult, have become little more than a chequered border.

Despite the black wing buds changing to a rich reddish brown, the adult *Piezodorus literatus* is still recogniseable from its overall greenish speckled appearance.

Although the duration of each nymphal stage can vary significantly, the development of this individual is consistent and barely another fortnight passes until its final moult. The mature adult has replaced blacks with reds and reds with pale greens. The transformation is remarkable, but when compared with its last few incarnations due to the dominant colours and texture, it is nevertheless recogniseable as the same species. Possibly the aspect of greatest significance is that whilst it bears no resemblance to the orange and black pin-head which emerged from its egg, this first-instar livery is a recurring theme across many different species of pentatomid.

Left: As hatching approaches, *Carpocoris purpureipennis* eggs (with millimetre markings) become more transparent.

Right: For a brief period the newly emerged hatchlings are vibrant orange with virtually no discernable markings.

Below: The eggs of *Dolycoris baccarum* show just how difficult it can be to identify some species in early stages.

To illustrate just how confusing shield bugs can be, above and below left are two egg clusters. The brighter orange of those above is due to their becoming more transparent as they come closer to hatching, yet both clusters are of entirely different species: *Carpocoris purpureipennis* (above) and *Dolycoris baccarum* (below). Comparing the two, the texture of the *Carpocoris* eggs above is less random, forming loose circles and the white ring is more pronounced. Otherwise they are strikingly similar considering that the adults are not, with *Dolycoris* resulting in a much more sombre-coloured adult.

We saw with the developing *Piezodorus*

Left: During the first hour after hatching the markings appear and darken.

Right: Twenty four hours later and the bright orange and black pattern is now clearly defined.

literatus that whilst there were significant changes, certain characteristics remained consistent from the third instar onwards. In other species no such consistency arises. The sequence above shows *Carpocoris purpureipennis* nymphs during their first fragile hours from hatching. Despite the orange ovals being quite unlike the grey and white, drum-shaped eggs of *Piezodorus literatus*, the emerging first-instar nymphs of both species appear remarkably similar. As they emerge from their eggs, the bright orange hatchlings remain huddled together, gradually darkening to reveal the familiar colouration of black pronotum with orange and black abdomen.

Over the next hour or so, the markings become fully defined and the tiny nymphs will remain clustered together on the eggs for days.

At least in some pentatomid species, when laying the eggs, the mother secretes tiny capsules containing a friendly bacteria which helps the nymphs' digestive systems break down their food. Although it is impossible to be certain, it seems likely that this is the case with the egg cluster on these pages as the nymphs remained on and around the eggs for more than a week. In fact, whilst a couple were adventurous enough to walk up and down the grass stem, the majority didn't move from the eggs at all during this time.

Above: For the second instar nymph, the initial orange skin transforms into more clearly defined markings.

Opposite: Ten days old and the *Carpocoris purpureipennis* nymphs have barely moved. Secreted bacteria left on and around the eggs by the mother provides some essential nutrition and one nymph has even managed to gain enough sustenance to grow into its second instar and sits beside the empty husk of its shed skin.

It seems remarkable that not only do the eggs provide enough sustenance to satisfy the nymphs for a full ten days, but one individual has managed to take in sufficient food to undergo its first moult, barely having wandered a centimetre and is nearly twice the size of its siblings. The huge growth rate from one instar to the next is clear to see. Bearing in mind that all the nymphs hatched within hours of each other, it barely seems possible that the soft orange body managed to remain in its old skin so long. Sitting beside its split exuvium, the second-instar nymph expands itself with air and body fluids, gradually hardening and darkening as fresh markings appear once again.

It is normal with shield bugs for the nymphs to remain together during their first and sometimes second instars. After this they will become progressively more solitary as they wander in search of fresh plants.

Above: Patterning on the speckled third-instar nymph is more starkly defined.

Opposite: As the fourth-instar nymph emerges from its old skin, an even greater change has occurred.

Two weeks later it has moulted again and aside from being larger, the third instar nymph has changed comparatively little. The pronotum has acquired a couple of white spots and the orange pigment of the abdomen has all but disappeared, leaving a more starkly red, white and black individual. The subtle signs of wing buds are just beginning to appear and now, at a little less than five millimetres long, since hatching it has grown to more than four times its original size.

It is from this point onwards that the changes become less predictable. A further two weeks pass and the nymph suspends itself again in preparation for the next moult. Pigmentation always takes some time to stabilise as the fresh exoskeleton dries and hardens. The initial colour is always orange as the nymphs shed each skin but even as it moults for the third time and the fourth-instar nymph emerges, it is clear to see that the markings have undergone more dramatic changes.

Above: The fourth-instar *Carpocoris purpureipennis* nymph has developed a much brighter and more colourful appearance.

Left and opposite: The emerging fifth-instar has changed again. The patterning is more intricate and the wing buds are now very clearly defined. As with all the moults so far, the markings start as a general pinky-orange pigment and we must wait a couple of hours to see how they will stabilise.

The head, once black, now carries two white stripes, and the pronotum's two white spots have made way for a more intricate pattern of black and white. The remaining red of the abdomen has become little more than a stripe, the wing buds are much more distinct and even the legs have undergone a complete transformation. Only the tarsi are black, with tibiae now yellow and femora white, altogether a much brighter colouration.

Closer to three weeks pass before the next moult and this time it is as if a completely different creature has taken its place. As the fifth-instar nymph emerges, at first it seems reasonably similar, other than the patterning being more intricate and the wing buds now extending beyond the pronotum, over the first abdominal segments. As the pigmentation stabilises, virtually nothing familiar remains.

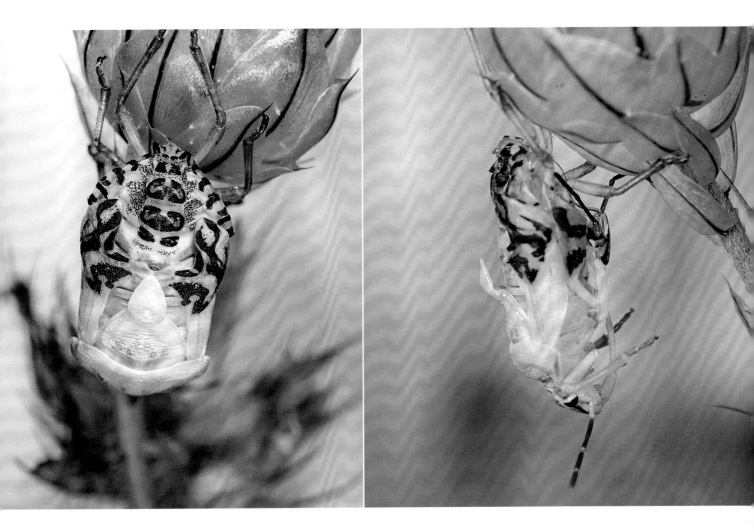

Opposite: Another remarkable transformation reveals a fifth-instar nymph looking completely unlike its old self.

Above: Nearly three weeks pass until the final moult and a very different looking adult emerges.

All that remains of the previous coloration is the faintest tinge of red across the abdomen. The stark white has become more creamy in hue, spots and stripes of black and red are now a slightly iridescent brown, even the yellow socks have disappeared in favour of a more uniform speckled white.

How evolution gave rise to such inconsistency is a mystery but the show is far from over. A few weeks later when the winged adult bursts out of its fifth instar skin, it has not even kept the familiar temporary coat of orange. This time, a pale yellow body emerges, with a splash of red here and there and visually, hardly a thing to connect it with the torn, shed exuvium. The duration of the moult itself can vary from minutes to half an hour or so, largely depending on humidity and how easy it is for the bug to ease itself out of the old exoskeleton.

Above: As usual, the pigmentation takes time to appear. Half an hour later the fresh exoskeleton has lost its wrinkles and brown markings begin to appear. After two hours the brown has become black and the wing tips are now clearly visible.

Opposite: Depending on conditions, the final pigmentation may take up to four days to appear. In this case, just two days later, the simple cream and black has transformed into reds and golds.

Over the next couple of hours the *Carpocoris* adult's final exoskeleton inflates and hardens, first becoming a paler creamy yellow as the wrinkles disappear. The reds darken from browns to blacks and gradually develop an overall mottled black patterning. The long triangular scutellum now extends way down the abdomen as if pointing to the darkened membranous tips of the hind wings.

It takes a full two to three days for the pigmentation to stabilise and the final adult form is an elegant blend of blacks, reds and yellows, a far cry from the brown and white fifth instar. As a species, *Carpocoris purpureipennis* with its the constantly evolving array of colours must rate as one of the greatest costume-changers of the natural world.

NEUROPTERA

Lacewings and their relatives

Neuroptera, the nerve winged, is the first of the holometabolous orders to be explored here. Complete metamorphosis, the development of a larva which bears no resemblance to its adult form, appears later in the fossil record, so these orders are considered to be 'higher' or more evolved. Essentially, a larva could be described as a free living embryo and these shape-shifting life cycles became so successful that they now account for a vast percentage of all species on earth.

The larvae of all the neuropterans are predatory and the huge majority remain so as adults. Many are fairly weak in flight but some, such as the ascalaphid *Libelloides coccajus* (opposite), are powerful predators, plucking their prey out of the air at lightning speeds.

Above and below: Lacewing eggs are laid in varying numbers. Some species lay individually, others in large clusters, sometimes as many as 50 or more.

Opposite: A mating pair of *Libelloides coccajus*. These ascalaphids are amongst the order's powerful fliers.

Left: After two weeks, a row of five eggs hatch within an hour of each other.

Above: The eggs of different lacewing species are laid in a huge variety of patterns. Singly, clustered, in rows or in circles, it remains extremely difficult to identify each species.

There are many extraordinary features within the order but few can be as remarkable as the sheer beauty and delicacy of lacewings' eggs. Laid singly or in large clusters, these tiny, mysterious, long-stemmed pods seem so alien that even today, in some parts of the world there are people who believe them to be the minuscule flowers of a magical plant. The fragile-looking, yet remarkably strong structures are created by the female touching her abdomen to the chosen surface and pulling away to leave the egg suspended on the end of a long, quick-drying stalk.

Above: Newly hatched larvae of green lacewings are quite unpredictable and may remain clinging to their eggs for a few minutes or more than a day.

The eggs themselves are generally around one millimetre in length and, depending on species and temperature, hatch after three days to two weeks. Seeming to darken as hatching approaches, as is commonly the case with insect eggs, the darkening is actually the egg becoming transparent, revealing the shadowy form of the developing larva within.

Sometimes they remain clinging to their eggs for as long as two days, perhaps until hunger forces them into action. Others climb down the silken strand almost immediately but then seem to do little more than walk some distance back and forth for several hours. However, when they do set off on their predacious life style, they are astonishing in their proficiency and some species are so voracious that they are reared commercially for use in pest control.

The fearsome-looking fangs are sharp tubes, through which they first inject digestive enzymes,

Above: The empty corpses of their victims are used as camouflage and piled up into their dorsal hairs.

Below: In the absence of corpses, early instars may camouflage themselves with scraps of vegetation.

before sucking out the dissolved innards from their prey. As they grow, the larvae camouflage themselves under growing piles of the remains of their prey, securely hooked into their long dorsal hairs. This urge to camouflage is strongly hard-wired and early instars may even use odd bits of vegetation, particularly after a moult when the previous stack of corpses has fallen off.

The larvae pass through three instars in two to three weeks before spinning a cocoon. Some

Above: The adult will shed its pupal skin as it emerges from the cocoon.

Right: An adult Chrysoperla. Many species of this genus are so alike that the only way to tell them apart is through their mating song. Each species uses a different vibrational pattern.

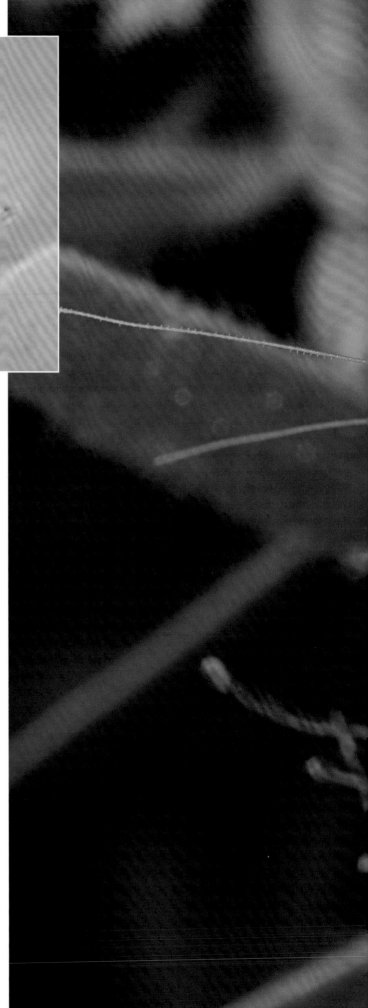

species camouflage the cocoon by spinning the silk into scraps of vegetation.

Pupation is fairly rapid. The adults emerge after around a week, although later in the year they will overwinter in the cocoon, and emerge in the spring. Adults emerging late in the year will hibernate in sheltered spots or leaf litter, sometimes waking and taking to the air on warm winter days.

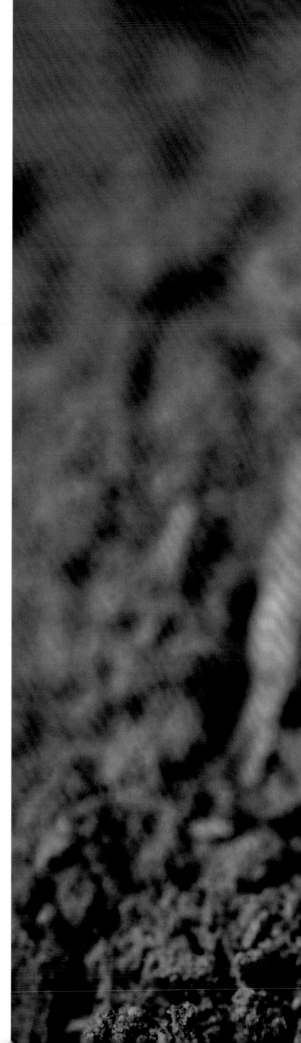

The larvae of Myrmeleontids, the antlions, are arguably the stuff of nightmares when viewed in close-up. Sometimes called doodlebugs, after the wiggly lines they make in the soil when moving to fresh territory, some species of these demonic-looking creatures dig pitfall traps in dry sandy soil to catch their prey. Here they lie hidden, buried at the bottom of the trap... waiting.

They create the conical pits by working their way backwards in decreasing circles, spiralling downwards, allowing the natural slip of the sand grains to define the depth. At the bottom, they lie in the soil to one side of the pit, with just head and fangs protruding into the trap itself.

Above: Once caught between the antlion's fearsome jaws, prey are quickly subdued.

Left: An escaping ant is bombarded with a deluge of sand as the antlion larva tries to knock it back down into the trap.

When an ant stumbles into the pit, on rare occasions it may slip straight into the antlion's waiting jaws. If not, all hell breaks loose. As the panicking ant tries to escape, the sand collapses underneath it, over and over again, bringing it back down into the trap. If stronger individuals manage to reach higher up the walls, the antlion tosses its head repeatedly, sending explosions of sand upwards to knock the prey back down to its waiting jaws. Once caught, they are quickly subdued and pulled beneath the surface to be sucked dry.

Above: Cleaned of soil to show the characteristic larval form.

Below: A second- instar larva (with millimetre markings) showing how the body hairs hold on to sand.

Antlion larvae are covered in spiny hairs which help them to remain stable in the loose sand. It also makes them difficult to see in the soil and I confess to feeling slightly guilty when taking the photograph above in order to show their morphology more clearly. They really do not appreciate being removed from the soil and cleaned.

Although ants are the most common prey, the larvae will eat anything suitable which falls into

Above: A discarded moult showing how the new instar emerges through a split at the thorax.

the trap. Due to their tiny size, early instars are often not strong enough to catch and subdue much prey. This problem is compounded by the fact that their proportionately tiny pits will only ensnare the tiniest of creatures, as most others simply walk straight over the top of them.

This hit-and-miss method of feeding makes the life cycles of pit-building Myrmeleontidae quite unpredictable and it is not uncommon for them to spend two years in the ground.

Like their lacewing cousins, the antlions pass through three instars but with the pit-dwellers, moulting takes place under the soil. The old skin splits across the thorax and when the emerging instar has pushed itself free, it will rest to allow the new exoskeleton to dry and harden before tossing the exuvium out of the pit. A careful search around their pits may reveal a couple of different-sized moults in amongst the thrown-out remains of the insects' previous victims.

Although, as previously mentioned, a larval period of two years is not uncommon, in areas where food is plentiful, antlions may reach adulthood in a matter of months. Pit building or repair is mostly carried out under cover of darkness, as is relocation. However, this does not mean that the larvae are nocturnal. In fact, they seem eternally ready to grasp prey at any time of day or night.

When pupation approaches, the larva stops eating and collapses the pit, bringing the soil down on top of itself. A few days pass, sometimes as long as a week, before the larva creates a spherical cocoon the size of a large pea, by binding grains of sand together with saliva. The adult emerges around 30 days later, always during the night, shedding the last moult as it makes its way out of the cocoon. Making its way upwards, it breaks free from the soil and searches for somewhere suitable to climb that will provide enough space for it to expand and dry its long and slender wings.

Left to right: Usually around 1cm in diameter antlions construct their cocoons by mixing sand and saliva. It will be around four weeks before the adult emerges.

An excavated specimen shows how, whilst still beneath the soil, the adult sheds its pupal skin as it emerges from the cocoon.

Under the cover of darkness, the adult struggles to the surface and immediately climbs something close by, which offers sufficient height for the long and delicate wings to expand and harden.

Left to right: Emerging antlions expand their wings quickly. Just ten minutes separate these pictures.

Expanding the wings happens remarkably quickly, these three photographs were taken in the space of just ten minutes. Something almost impossible to see once the wings have reached their full size, is the delicate colouring of yellows, greens and blues which fade away by the minute.

It takes a further ten minutes for the wings to reach their full length and an hour or two more for the fresh exoskeleton to harden. Then, depending on conditions, they may fly off in search of more suitable shelter, or spend more time cleaning off the remaining powdery sand.

Without the sandy coating, the distinctive clubbed antennae and complex mouth parts are much easier to see, as are the enormous bulging eyes. There are a number of similar-looking species, most commonly distinguished by their venation and wing markings (or lack of them). Fully expanded, the markings reveal this to be *Euroleon nostras*. Weak and fluttery in flight, after two years in the ground, this nocturnal adult may live just four or five weeks.

Euroleon nostras, identified by its wing markings. Some similar looking species have no dark spots at all and are distinguished by the unique pattern of their venation.

COLEOPTERA

Beetles form the largest order of all insects, comprising more than 350,000 known species across more than 170 families, accounting for more than a third of all known insect species. Their adaptability in evolutionary terms has enabled them to inhabit almost every environment on earth, with species feeding on anything imaginable. Carnivores, vegetarians and scavengers consume everything from live prey and rotting corpses to fresh green shoots, fungi and decomposing wood. Many, such as weevils (which account for around 14 per cent of all beetles), are serious plant pests. Others, like the carrion-feeding Silphidae, are important decomposers, playing an essential role in maintaining healthy ecosystems.

The principal characteristic of almost all beetles is that the forewings have evolved to become hardened protective shields, called elytra, which cover the hind wings when at rest. Usually the elytra cover the entire abdomen, but in some groups, such as the oil beetles (Meloidae) and rove beetles (Staphylinidae) they are very short, leaving the abdomen exposed.

Gonioctena (right), a genus of the leaf beetle family (Chrysomelidae) is one of the few groups which give birth to live young. Parental care is unusual, the vast majority laying eggs and leaving the young to fend for themselves. Some however, are devoted and highly protective parents, seeing their young into

Above: The different colouration of this mating pair of Gonioctena leaf beetles show the clear sexual dimorphism in this genus. These beetles are unusual in giving birth to live young.

Opposite: Acorn Weevils, *Curculio venosus*, lay their eggs inside acorns where the larvae develop until autumn. When the acorn falls to the ground the larva gnaws an exit hole and burrows into the soil to pupate.

Above: Cerambycid larvae chew long tunnels as they eat their way through timber. They are easily recognised by their distinctive tapered body shape.

adulthood. Worthy of mention are the Passalidae, which not only live in family units, rearing their young and helping the larvae to construct their pupal case, they also communicate with a 'vocabulary' of distinct sounds.

Typically, Coleoptera larvae will undergo three or four moults before reaching the pupal stage but for some species the number of instars is much higher. Larvae of the tenebrionid *Tribolium*

casteneum, the Red Flour Beetle, can moult between five and 11 times in a matter of weeks before pupation. As an adult, this serious food pest can then go on to live for more than three years.

The variation in size is enormous, ranging from some flower beetles at under half a millimetre to giants such as *Titanus giganteus* from South America, which measures up to 170mm. But perhaps a more remarkable aspect, setting

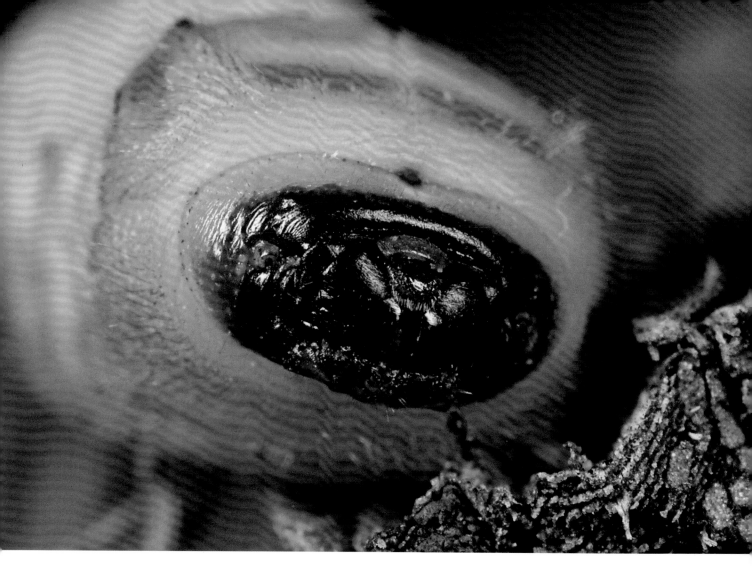

Above: With immensely powerful jaws,
Longhorn larvae are able to gnaw through the
hardest wood.

Coleoptera apart from the majority of other insects, is the wide variation in the duration of larval development. The juvenile stages of beetles' lives can range from a few weeks in many species to decades in some of the wood-boring beetles. The larvae of most longhorn beetles (Cerambycidae) for example, feed on living or dead wood and have evolved powerful jaws which enable them to chew tunnels through the toughest of timbers. These wood-borers manage to extract enough benefit to avoid starvation, but with a diet of such low nutritional value, it is no surprise that development can be extremely slow.

Despite the limited diet however, most Cerambycidae reach adulthood in one to two years and whilst feeding on wood may not be particularly nutritious, it is an eternally abundant food source. Another advantage to the longhorn

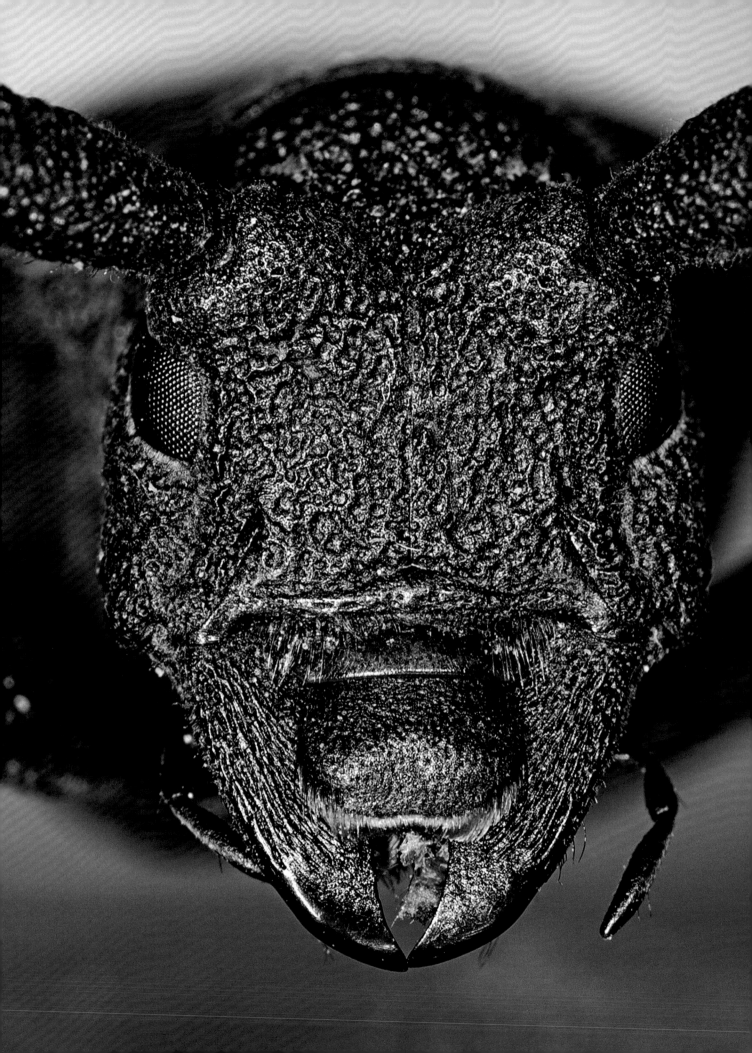

Above: A longhorn pupates inside its timber home without the need of a protective cocoon.

Left: A Cerambyx scopolii showing the equally impressive adult jaws. This individual is chewing a nettle leaf.

lifecycle is that, being hidden away inside solid wood, the risk of predation is hugely reduced. Indeed, the environment is so constant that many species have evolved to pupate without the need of a protective cocoon.

Interestingly, even when they have left their wood chewing days behind, their jaws become no less impressive, despite the fact that as adults the majority of species depend on much softer diets of leaves, sap, fungi and flowers.

Above: The beautiful *Lilioceris lilii* can be a real garden pest. Larvae and adults both feed exclusively on lilies.

Opposite: Resting on the underside of a lily leaf, the brightly coloured eggs of *Lilioceris lilii*, just 1mm long, will hatch after around three weeks.

Leaf Beetles (Chrysomelidae), with over 35,000 species, form one of the largest of the beetle families which, in varying degrees, consume leaves and other plant material. Some are fairly unfussy eaters but others are real specialists, feeding on very particular food plants. One such specialist is the Scarlet Lily beetle *(Lilioceris lilii)* which, as the name implies, feeds solely on the fleshy leaves of the lily family.

The bright red eggs are laid on the underside of leaves, usually in clusters of half a dozen or so.

Gestation periods range from as little as one week to as long as a month. Like most things in the insect world, factors such as temperature and humidity play their part. Normally insects hatch faster in warm conditions but of the numerous clutches I have observed, some have emerged after a month in warm, sunny weather. However, the fastest hatchers, emerging after one week, were laid during a particularly cold and wet month of May, so clearly there are other, more subtle factors affecting the length of their development.

Above: A tiny Scarlet Lily Beetle larva breaks free from its egg.

Below: As soon as they hatch, these ravenous creatures begin eating.

When they hatch, these tiny, transluscent larvae are around one millimetre in length, but growth is fast due to the very aspect which causes them to be so hated by gardeners: they consume lily leaves at an astonishing rate. Within 15 minutes of hatching, this tiny, wrinkled larva has already eaten a hole the size of its head. Only hours later, their bodies have visibly distended and they are already beginning to accumulate a characteristic faecal shield.

The use of faeces as defence is common to a number of beetle species and seems to serve different functions. The accumulated pile darkens

Above: Twelve hours later and already, patches of flesh have been stripped right down to the leaf's tougher cuticle.

Below: At two days old the larvae have produced enough faeces to be almost completely covered.

as it hardens and acts very effectively as a predator deterrent. Other than the obvious aspect of camouflage, ants in particular find the shields repellent and actively avoid touching them. If they do unintentionally make contact with the noxious goo, they retreat immediately and clean themselves as if it was truly disgusting.

Rolling the faeces upwards with muscular contractions, the larvae keep piling them on to reach improbable heights. Sometimes the shield gets knocked off if, for example, a larva attempts to squeeze through too small a gap between leaves. Otherwise the pile will accumulate until either it

Above: The second-instar larvae have filled out and continue to graze together.

Left: By the third instar, the faecal shield, if it has not been shed or dislodged, begins to develop a crust.

Above right: A seemingly impossible feat, the larva sheds a skin whilst retaining its faecal shield. The fresh-faced fourth instar is yet to develop its darker pigment and the dark legs and head capsule of the previous skin can be seen in the background. Looking quite precarious, the old, crusty coating of faeces now extends well over the head and all the time the larva just keeps eating.

becomes too heavy and falls away, or the load is shed with a moult.

Growth continues at a remarkable rate with each instar lasting less than a week. In the early stages, the larvae consume only the flesh of the leaves, leaving the tough, transparent cuticle, hanging limply from the stems. After the second moult however, the larger, third-instar larvae begin to consume the leaves in their entirety.

Most insects have a brief period of inactivity either side of a moult as they first loosen the new, unexposed skin from the old and afterwards, wait for the new skin to dry and harden. Not so Scarlet Lily Beetles. Even as the skin is shed they continue chomping away, sometimes even managing to moult without losing the crusted fecal shield. Above, an emerging fourth-instar larva has eased itself out of the third-instar skin whilst simultaneously eating and nudging the gooey mass forwards. The dark legs and head-capsule of the old exuvium are still partially attached and visible towards the rear of the abdomen.

Above: Beneath a cracked faecal shield, a fourth-instar larva reveals its more elongated body shape.

Below: When viewed from below, it is easier to see how the larval skin splits and falls away during a moult.

Very occasionally a larva is so successful at keeping hold of a shield that it even lasts long enough to grow mould. At this stage though, the crustiness makes the pile so inflexible that it can crack and drop away in pieces. The larva above, having lost a sizeable chunk of its faecal shield, reveals the more elongated body shape of the fourth and final instar.

After the fourth moult everything changes. The pupa is altogether darker and now, in a non-feeding phase, the skin appears drier and tougher.

Above: The non-feeding pupa spends its time in polarised behaviour, either completely inactive or wandering restlessly.

Below: Climbing down the stem, the pupa will search for a suitable place to burrow into the ground.

A seemingly confused and restless period follows, as if, having stopped eating for the first time since hatching, it has absolutely no idea what to do with itself. The pupa begins to spend long periods almost motionless, followed by spells of almost frantic pacing.

Actual pupation takes place in the soil and the pupa will climb down the plant stem and begin searching for a suitable place to bury itself. This appears to be another period of indecision and, on more than one occasion, I have observed a pupa

Above: Many hours may be spent looking for a suitable place to pupate.

Below: Digging in, the pupa will excavate a neat burrow before it begins constructing its cocoon.

search the soil for hours, only to climb back up the plant stem and remain there for a further day or two.

Once the decision has been made and it has buried itself a small way into the ground, the pupa will begin to create a froth of saliva which it will mix with grains of soil, gradually building up an even, spherical cocoon. Inside this protective ball, the remarkable transformation from a soft, fleshy juvenile to the fully armoured adult form begins

Above: Mixing saliva and soil, the pupa creates a frothy mass from which it will construct the cocoon.

Below: The clay cocoon sticks neatly to the pupa. A spot of the adult's red carapace is exposed on the left-hand side.

to take place within the pupal skin. After between two and three weeks the developed adult breaks free from the old skin and chews its way out of the cocoon. It is actually the shedding of the old skin that gives the adult the freedom to move again, as the saliva-soil mixture creates a sort of clay which sticks strongly to the pupa's skin.

It is worth making a comparison here with another species which undergoes a similar process of pupation, but with a slight difference for the

Above: A rose chafer pupates with plenty of room to move within its cocoon.

Below: Adult rose chafers grazing on lilac.

emerging adult. Like the Scarlet Lily Beetle, the Rose Chafer, (*Cetonia aurata*) from the family Scarabaeidae constructs its cocoon by mixing soil and saliva into a clay. However the chafer pupa leaves itself room to move inside the hollow ball, which reduces the risks to the developing adult should the cocoon be damaged.

The pupal stage of scarabaeids is much closer to the final adult form and, as the skin is not attached to the wall of the cocoon as it is with the Scarlet Lily Beetle, the last moult may occur some days before the mature beetle breaks free.

The adult emerges, days after its final moult inside the cocoon.

DIPTERA

The true flies

The most distinguishing feature of the true flies, separating them from all other fly-like insects, is the presence of halteres. These small, teardrop shaped balancing organs are a reduced pair of wings, where evolution has favoured the increase in flying agility provided by replacing one pair, usually the hind-wings, with what are essentially miniature gyroscopes. Diptera first appeared some 240 million years ago during the Triassic era and this new found flying agility with increased capability for predator evasion, gave rise to an immense diversity. It is probably fair to say that to most people, the word 'fly' conjours up images of bluebottles, fruit flies and white maggots but Diptera opens up a Pandora's box of variety in form and behaviour. The size of halteres varies greatly between species and has little or no bearing on the size of the fly itself. As always, size isn't everything.

There are more than 120,000 known species, roughly a quarter of which have been identified and described since the late 1980s. They range from tiny species such as the gall midges (Cecidomyiidae), some of which are sub-millimetre, to the enormous *Gaudomyras heros* of the family Mydidae. This giant can reach 6cm in length with a wingspan of 10cm.

Strictly speaking, Diptera are divided into two suborders identified by their antennae: Nematocera (thread-horned) and Brachycera (short-horned). The difference is clearly visible in the amber-trapped Fungus Gnat (left) and Horse Fly (above). It can seem a little confusing that Brachycera are further divided into two groups: Orthorrhapha and Cyclorrhapha. The main distinction of Cyclorrhapha is straightforward: the adult emerges

Above: A clear example of Brachycera. The short antennae of Horse Flies (Tabanidae) are situated below the large eyes, which are often brilliantly coloured, as seen in this *Hybomitra micans*.

Opposite: A Fungus Gnat (Mycetophylidae) trapped in Baltic amber, 55 million years old, is easily recognised as a thread-horned Nematoceran.

through a circular opening in the pupal case.
Orthorrapha however, cannot be defined so simply.
One principal characteristic is that the pupa
emerges from the last larval skin via a T-shaped
split in the back, although this obviously won't be
of any use when attempting to identify an adult in
the field. Differences between Orthorrhapha and
Cyclorrhapha are only really distinct in their
larval stages, the simplest being that
Orthorrhapha do not create a pupal case.

A small percentage of Diptera have fully
aquatic larvae, the best known being mosquitoes
(Culicidae), of which there are roughly 3,000
described species worldwide, divided into two
groups: culicines and anophelines. Anophelines
are the malaria carriers, identified by their bodies
being tilted at an angle with head downwards
when at rest. Culicines hold their bodies
horizontally or with head tilting upwards. So
whilst you may not want to be bitten by either, you
are more likely to get a decent night's sleep when
you can recognise the differences.

Only females bite, the blood diet providing
proteins for the production of healthy eggs.

Below: Male mosquitoes are easily
distinguished from females by their bushy palps
and antennae.

Opposite: After struggling to free herself from
her pupal skin, a newly emerged adult female
Culex pipiens rests on the water surface as her
wings harden.

Above: Mosquito larvae grow from tiny 2mm long, transparent hatchlings to opaque, wide-eyed fourth instars 10mm or so in length.

otherwise. both sexes are nectar feeders. Males are distinguished by their hairy antennae and palps.

Perhaps surprisingly, despite the fact that the larvae need an environment of still water to complete their life-cycle, they are also found in the most arid environments where the eggs can remain dormant for long periods, waiting until water levels rise sufficiently for development. Once the eggs hatch however. complete metamorphosis usually takes only three to four weeks, with four larval instars before emerging as a pupa after the fourth moult. *Culex pipiens* shown here, is an abundant species, and as with all mosquitoes. the larvae graze on microscopic algae and bacteria,

filtering their food through brush-like hairs around their mouths. Mosquito larvae breathe air through a tubelike appendage, called a syphon, extending upwards from the end of the abdomen. Below the syphon a pair of tracheal gills protrude downwards, extracting oxygen from the water.

First-instar larvae are tiny, just a couple of millimetres in length and almost glass-like in transparency. As they grow the changes are subtle. They become slightly more opaque with each moult and seem to grow into the tufts and hairs which protrude from each body segment. By the fourth instar the thorax has become opaque white and the eyes have grown considerably.

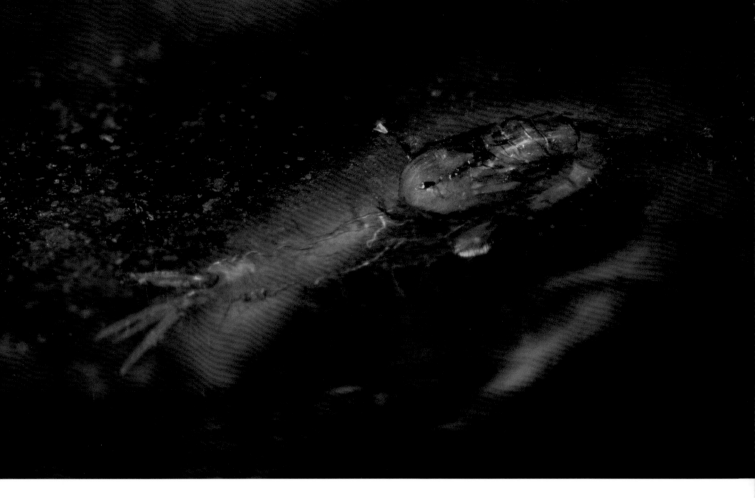

Above: A fourth-instar larva moults into its
agile-swimming pupal form.

Most of their time is spent floating just below
the surface with only the syphon's tip exposed to
the air. They are however, extremely mobile,
swimming freely to reach a new source of food.
When the need arises they can also be astonishigly
fast, darting away when startled by potential
predators or, frustratingly, the shadows of careless
photographers who haven't paid attention to the
sun's position in the sky.

The drama really begins after the fourth moult
when the pupa emerges from the last larval skin
with an entirely new body form. The most
remarkable changes are that the syphon is
replaced by two breathing tubes called respiratory
trumpets which are now situated above the head
on the cephalothorax, and the tracheal gills have
become paddle-shaped, looking rather like
miniature whale flukes. This non-feeding stage
lasts a few days but the pupa has lost none of its
larval mobility. The new paddle-shaped tail can
propel it through the water with remarkable speed
when disturbed. Most of the time however, it will
waste no energy, preferring to float motionless, like
an inflated comma, as its adult form continues to
develop. During the next couple of days, under
this short-lived skin, the adult features become
increasingly visible in what appears to be a tangle
of legs and antennae.

Towards the end of pupation, adult features such as compound eyes and segmented antennae are well developed and now clearly visible.

At the end of pupation the adult body looks as if it could simply burst out of the pupal skin but its emergence is as graceful as it is urgent. When development is complete the pupa begins to straighten out, lying almost flat at the water surface, wriggling gently to loosen itself from the old skin. Of around 30 mosquitoes I watched through their development, most took approximately one hour to uncurl themselves and sometimes several hours to separate themselves inside the old skin. This seems to depend entirely on the individual as some were faster and others slower, in identical conditions. It seems likely that this depends largely on the amount of energy they

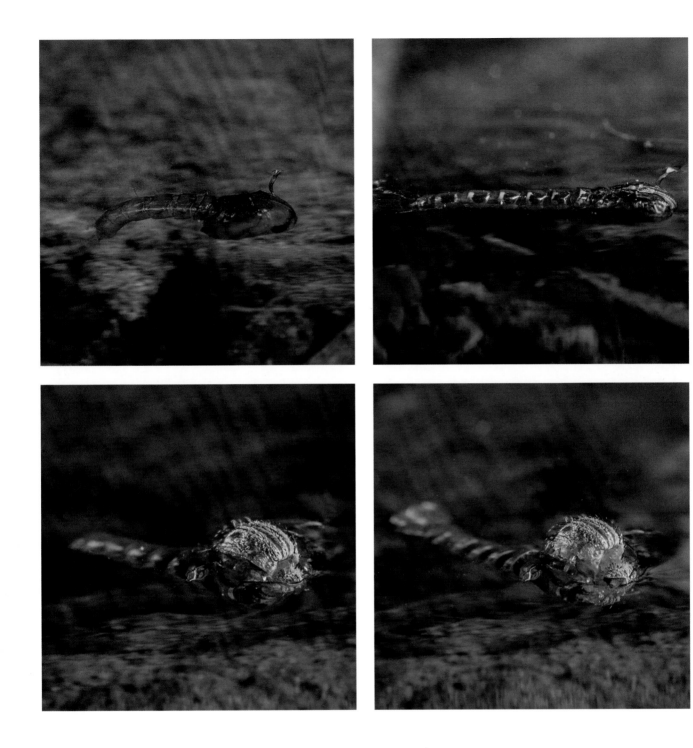

have left from feeding during the larval stage. Once fully uncurled, a split begins to appear in the cephalothorax and the adult pushes itself upwards through the hole, using its old skin as a raft during the most vulnerable part of its development. The effort is intense as the soft, fragile body continues to rise from the water.

Top left: The pupa uncurls its body to lie flat along the water surface.

Top right: After a period of wriggling to loosen the old skin, a split appears in the cephalothorax.

Below left: The adult begins to force itself upward through the split.

Below right: Within minutes, the bright compound eyes begin to break the surface.

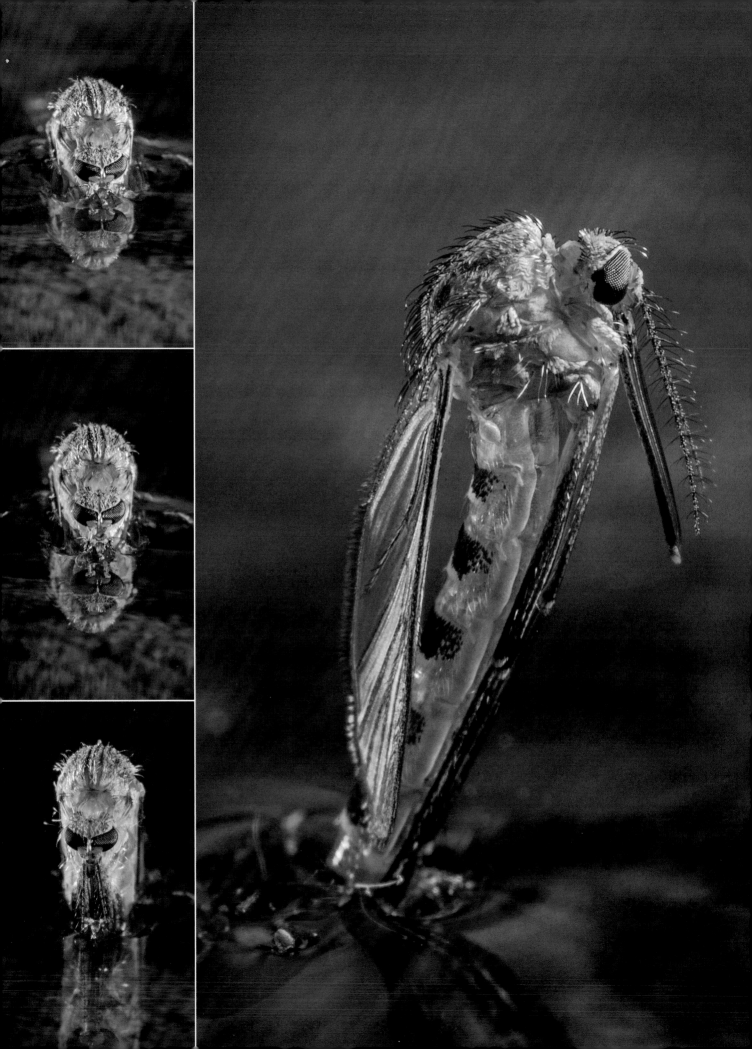

Opposite: As the head and thorax break the surface and she strains to free her legs this female mosquito provides a perfect view of a Diptera-defining haltere just below the base of the wings.

Above: Once her legs are free she can stand on the water surface and complete the moult more easily.

Below: Unable to pull its legs free from the pupal skin, this individual has died in the first moments of adulthood.

As the head emerges it is clear for the first time from the lightly haired antennae and hairless mouthparts that this is a female. Legs pulled taut as she continues to push, it is only when they are pulled free that she can lower herself to stand on the water surface. Here, she will allow her skin and wings to harden before flying off in search of a mate.

A life cycle requiring the shift from water-dwelling larva to airborne adult illustrates another aspect within the fragile lives of insects. Occasionally their legs become tangled as they try to exit the pupal skin. The more they struggle, the more tired they become, making it increasingly difficult to break free. Some even die of exhaustion in the attempt (right).

Overleaf: A pair of mating *Sphaerophoria* hover flies show a very different sexual dimorphism from the bushy or bald mosquito.

Here, colour as well as body shape is markedly different, the male on the left being more brightly coloured and with a longer, more slender abdomen.

Some species can be particularly difficult to identify or may even be missed completely, when superficially they resemble something familiar. The Sphaerophoria on the previous page are members of the family Syrphidae. Commonly called hoverflies, the family's 6000 or so species are a common sight worldwide, hanging in the air on sunny days.

From the pronounced haltere, the fly opposite is clearly another dipteran and would almost certainly be passed by as another species of slender hoverfly. But actually, this seemingly familiar creature is amongst the rarest and least understood of all the true flies. Vermileonidae, meaning worm lions, are named after the larvae, which construct pitfall traps to catch their prey. They are the only known family of flies to do this.

To give their rarity a little context, the 120,000 or so species of Diptera are divided into 130 families, and some of these families are vast. Tipulidae, the crane flies for example, includes more than 15,000 species, Drosophilidae, which include the fruit flies, number around 4,000, Tabanidae, the horse flies, around 4,500, and Syrphidae, as mentioned above, around 6,000. At the opposite end of the scale, there are numerous smaller families. The Trichoceridae or winter crane flies number around 160 species worldwide; Anisopodidae, the wood gnats, around 150. At the extreme end are families like the Axymyiidae with just a handful of species. In the face of these numbers it comes as no great surprise that Vermileonidae are so little known. Worldwide, the family contains just 60 to 80 species.

Vermileo vermileo, the more widely distributed species of Vermileonidae found in Europe.

Above: Pitfall traps of wormlions and antlions. All but two of these belong to wormlion larvae.

Below: The distinctly shaped and powerful tail of wormlion larvae.

The genus name *Vermileo*, or wormlion, is a clear reference to the more widely known pit-making behaviour of antlions. The significant difference is that antlions are named after their prey, wormlions are named after their appearance: they do not eat worms.

Aside from the name and pit-making behaviour, the only other similarity is habitat. Due to their need for dry, sheltered, powdery soil, wormlions are likely to be found sharing territory with antlions.

Above: A late instar larva, about 15mm long, showing its distinctly tapering shape.

Below: The posterior abdominal segments bear bristly hairs which help the larva anchor itself in the soil.

When this does occur, there will usually be a considerably higher percentage of wormlions to antlions. A close look reveals that their pits are very slightly different, essentially due to the manner of construction. Antlions crawl backwards in a descending spiral which creates a pit resembling a very even, inverted cone. Wormlion larvae create their pits by anchoring themselves in the substrate using the rows of stiff hairs on their rear abdominal segments. Then, by repeatedly flicking their heads,

Above: The first-instar larvae make tiny pits to catch their prey.

Below: *Monobella grassei*, a species of springtail shown at the same scale as the larva above, illustrates the sort of prey wormlion larvae may be able to catch.

they toss the grains of soil away. This usually results in fresh wormlion pits having slightly steeper sides than those of antlions.

It is unclear quite how soon after hatching the wormlion larvae begin to excavate pits, but certainly it cannot be long because they are absolutely tiny. When the pit is made, the larva lies with its abdomen upwards, ready to grab on to anything small enough to fall into the trap. It seems remarkable that a creature so small is capable of

Above: At the bottom of its pit, a second-instar larva lies in wait.

Below: The dark head capsule is completely retractable. Here, just the tip protrudes from the prothorax.

catching and subduing prey. The fact that there is anything small enough to be prey for the tiny first instars is just as remarkable and their diet most likely consists of other arthropods such as juvenile springtails (left) or barklice.

The dark head capsule can be completely retracted into the prothorax for protection, and sometimes, the larvae will seem to snuffle around with just the tip of their heads and their mouthparts exposed.

Above: Like lightning, the larva wraps itself round an ant which has stumbled into the pit.

Opposite: A bristly pseudopod just below the head helps the larva to grasp its prey.

The photograph opposite of a late instar shows first, how much the larvae grow over a period of months. The prothorax is nearly a millimetre across (the first instar on the previous page is shown between the millimetre markings). Second and more importantly, just below the head, is the wormlion's main weapon. A stubby protrusion, or pseudopod (so-called because it looks like a foot but isn't), bears a cluster of spiny hairs with which the larva can get a firm grip on its prey before sucking the living haemolymph out of it.

Perhaps the most significant disadvantage to this feeding behaviour is that meals may be few and far between. Anything from wind-blown leaves to larger creatures walking by, let alone unsuccessful struggles with potential prey, will cause the pit to collapse and require a large expenditure of energy to remake the trap. Also, the majority of suitable meals have the uncooperative tendency to simply walk around the pit.

The consequence of this hit-and-miss affair is that vermileonid life cycles can be as irregular as their

Above: When emergence is imminent, the pupa forces its way to the surface.

Opposite: The pupa will remain buried a centimetre or so below the surface for three to four weeks before the adult is ready to emerge.

meals. In my own research I found that some, like patient crocodiles, managed to survive months without eating but nevertheless, reacted immediately to an ant falling in the pit. Others died in identical conditions. Whatever the variables may be, it seems that, with a suitable supply of food, the larva reaches pupation in a single season. When prey is in short supply it may take two seasons in the ground to reach adulthood.

When pupation occurs it is dramatic. The larva collapses the pit, stops eating completely and remains a centimetre or so in the soil. The pupa develops in around ten days. The new soil-encrusted body shape is the complete opposite to its larval form. The slender head and thorax have become more pronounced with hints of the developing adult within and the powerful tail now has a slender, almost spring-like appearance. After a further three to four weeks, the pupa wriggles its way to the surface, possibly with the help of the curved tail, and rests in this position for anything up to two days. This totally irregular pause makes the actual emergence yet another unpredictable element of their life cycle but when ready, the pupal skin splits at the thorax and it is over in minutes.

Left: A split appears in the thorax as the adult begins to emerge.

Below and main picture: The adult has to expend enormous effort to free itself from the pupal skin. For this individual, the time from the split appearing to freedom was nine minutes.

Above: The newly emerged adult will rest for
an hour or two while her skin dries and hardens.

For *Vermileo vermileo*, emergence typically occurs early in the morning, not long after sunrise, although this may be different for other species. A ghostly pale adult clambers onto the soil, where it will move very little over the next few hours as its fresh exoskeleton dries and hardens.

The photograph above right, taken a day after the adult emerged from the soil, shows another side of their remarkable anatomy. When the exoskeleton has fully hardened and pigmentation stabilised, a broad white band is clearly visible, running the full length of the abdomen. This membrane, connecting the dorsal and ventral segments of the exoskeleton, provides the adult with vital flexibilty. This can be seen clearly in the photograph below right, showing another individual with the membrane contracted.

Also worthy of note and clear to see in the photograph of the stripeless male to the right, is that Vermileonidae have amongst the most pronounced halteres of all dipteran species.

Above: One day into adult life, the pigmentation reveals a white abdominal stripe. This expandable membrane gives us a glimpse into how the adult's tough exoskeleton can remain flexible.

Right: An individual showing the fully contracted membrane and the very prominent halteres.

LEPIDOPTERA

Butterflies and moths

It comes as a surprise to many that the distinction between butterflies and moths is far from straightforward, with no absolute rules or characteristics to separate one from the other. Rules of thumb should never be dismissed however, so if it forms its chrysalis openly on a food plant or suspended from a branch or convenient surface (above my kitchen door is a curiously frequent choice) it is almost certainly a butterfly. If, on the other hand, it spins itself a silk cocoon in which to pupate, it is certain to be a moth, but not all moths spin cocoons. The most obvious non-scientific rule of thumb is probably that butterflies are generally diurnal and brightly coloured, whilst moths are more commonly nocturnal and drably coloured. Worldwide there are in excess of 160,000 known species of Lepidoptera, around 90 percent of which are moths.

Whether butterfly or moth, their development follows the same overall sequence from caterpillar to winged adult with the skin being shed usually from three to five times. The sequence, however, comes in an astonishing wealth of variations. Some caterpillars hardly change at all from hatching to pupation. With others, at each moult the emerging instar becomes almost unrecognisable from the last.

Above: A Lappet Moth caterpillar chews its way out of its egg.

Opposite: Magnified more than 200 times, the beautiful iridescent scales of a South American *Morpho menelaus* butterfly.

Left and above: The stunning caterpillars of the saturniid moth *Dirphia avia*, from Central and South America, transform into rather drab adults. The caterpillars' fearsome-looking spines are a highly effective defence, delivering a painful sting if touched. The caterpillars are processionary and the individual opposite is in the process of feeding on the faeces of the sibling in front. Known as coprophagy, this is an efficient way of extracting the undigested nutrients which would otherwise be wasted.

Some butterflies and moths transform from dull larvae to brilliantly coloured adults, others, such as *Dirphia avia* shown here, are the complete opposite, with breathtaking larvae pupating into surprisingly sombre adulthood. More surprising in this species is that when pupation approaches, a cascade of hormones turns the larvae bright pink and they begin to pace restlessly, looking for a suitable place amongst the leaf litter to spin a cocoon. Inside the cocoon, they will gradually return to their original colour before actual pupation occurs.

Above: Surveying the world from a strand of fennel, a newly hatched European Swallowtail caterpillar rests beside an undeveloped egg.

Below: As hatching approaches, the egg becomes transparent to reveal the tiny larva within.

Whilst the impressive spines of *Dirphia avia* caterpillars are strongly poisonous, the larvae of a great many species may look dangerous but are often completely harmless. Mimicking the bright colours of poisonous species is another useful defence mechanism. Warning potential predators to keep away is a tactic used to good effect by many a harmless larva.

One highly inconsistent aspect amongst Lepidoptera is how larval coloration may or may

Above: The second instar swallowtail larva begins to gain more colour. The pronounced white, saddle-like marking is only present in the earlier instars.

not carry through to the adult form. As we saw with *Dirphia avia*, the adult shows no sign at all of its juvenile colouring. However, the early instars are the most variable, after which, in many species, the caterpillars can remain recognisable right through pupation.

A European Swallowtail (*Papilio machaon gorganus*) emerges from its egg as a tiny, greyish-black and spine-covered caterpillar. The first moult happens quite quickly and in just a few days, the second instar has emerged with a pronounced white saddle and orange spots around the spiracles. This apparent saddle of coloration is sometimes considered to have evolved as camouflage by its strong resemblance to bird droppings. This is far from certain however, as the colouration changes completely in the following instar, which would seem unlikely if the droppings resemblance did in fact hold any evolutionary advantage.

Above: Beside its shed second-instar skin, the caterpillar's huge growth rate is clearly apparent.

Opposite: These caterpillars consume the delicate fronds of umbelliferous plants at an astonishing rate.

Like most caterpillars, they feed voraciously and can develop through their early instars quite rapidly. Six days later, the second-instar larva moults into a much more striking individual. A slight trace of the pale saddle remains but the overall colouring has become an almost even balance of white, black and orange.

As the larvae grow bigger, so the duration of each instar grows longer. The total time taken from hatching, through five instars to the chrysalis, is normally between six and seven weeks. From the third instar onwards, the time between moults increases slightly, normally by a few days.

By the fourth instar, the coloration has become much more biased towards a pale ground with black and orange markings. At the fifth instar, the changes are more subtle, the most noticeable aspect being that the orange markings have reduced to slightly smaller spots.

The final larval stage for this individual lasts nine days. During this time it must gain as much weight as possible to fuel the huge amount of energy necessary for its approaching pupation. In this instar's later development, feeding stops and

Above: The fourth instar's overall colour is considerably paler. The glassy appearance of its face and transparency of its eyes show that the moult into the fifth and final instar has already begun.

Right: The fifth instar's fresh skin is clearly recognisable but the distribution of colour is slightly changed.

Inset: The face is almost colourless to begin with and it takes an hour or so for the black stripes to appear.

Above: Attached to its branch, when the chrysalis has formed, the last larval skin is shed in minutes.

Below: In contrast to the loose girdle of the swallowtail, the Black-veined White butterfly binds itself tightly in place.

the caterpillar may spend a couple of days looking for a suitable place to pupate. Once satisfied, the larva forms a silk pad on its chosen surface. Clasping on to this by its rear end, it then twists from side to side, spinning a silken girdle, securing itself upright with room to move.

An interesting contrast in this form of pupation is clear to see in the chrysalis shown left. Larvae of the Black-veined White butterfly (*Aporia crataegi*) bind a girdle so tight that it seems to almost cut into the chrysalis itself.

As the skin is shed, adult features are clearly
visible on the newly revealed chrysalis.

Once firmly secured, this pre-pupa stage
usually lasts two or three days, largely dependant
on temperature. During this time, inside the body
of the caterpillar the chrysalis is already
developing and when the final moult occurs it
happens very quickly. The wriggling pupa almost
bursts out of the swollen skin, revealing some
clearly recognisable adult features. Eyes,
antennae, proboscis and wings are clearly visible.
The sequence of four photographs above was
taken in less than two minutes.

Above and opposite: Almost eight months pass between the chrysalis forming and the adult emerging.

Below: A swallowtail chrysalis can remain almost white without surrounding colour to influence pigmentation.

With a final wriggle, the old skin is cast away and the chrysalis gradually darkens. This colouration will depend on its immediate environment with paler surroundings often giving rise to a green variant. In an experiment of my own, a European Swallowtail caterpillar allowed to pupate in a spacious tank secured itself to the glass wall. With no surrounding colour to influence its development, the resulting chrysalis remained unchanged (left).

Pupation times are hugely varied and late-summer larvae will commonly overwinter in this phase. For this individual, almost eight months elapsed between the photographs above, taken in early September, and the final emergence (opposite) at the end of the following March.

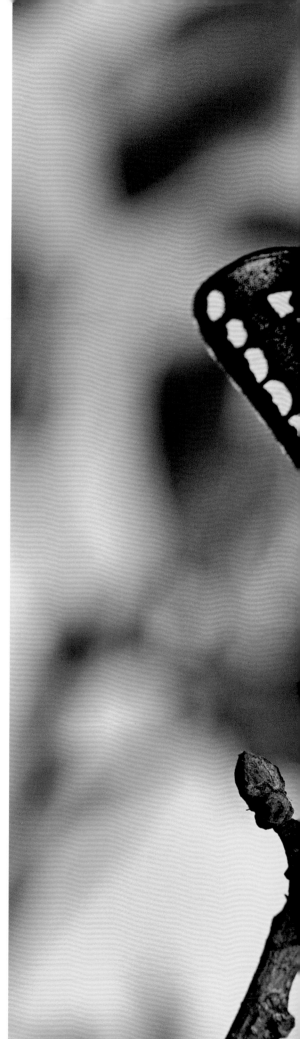

Expanding the wings by pumping fluids
through the veins, it will take the butterfly a
couple of hours to be ready for flight.

The newly emerged adult is at its most
vulnerable in the period immediately after
emergence. The crumpled wings must be pumped
full of haemolymph and allowed to harden, which
can take a few hours.

Butterflies are generally ready to mate as soon
as they have emerged and one difference between
the sexes is that once the wings have hardened, a
male will fly off almost immediately in search of a
partner. Females are more likely to wait to be
found. This individual remained on the same twig
for two days.

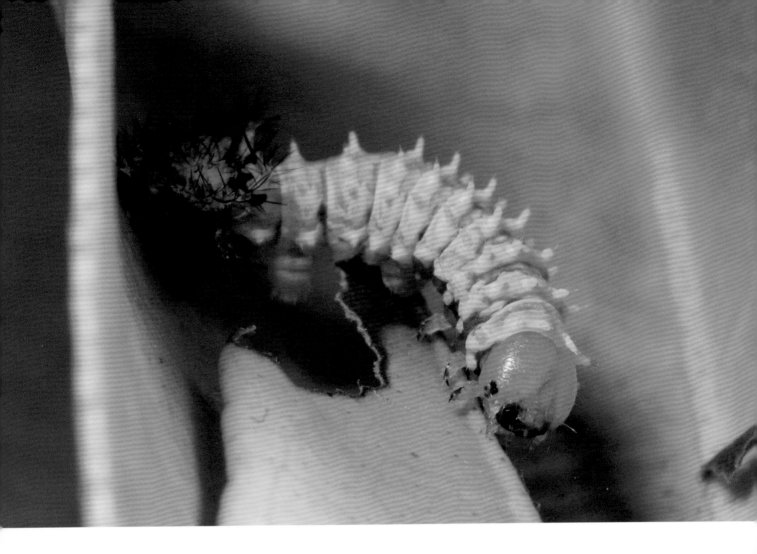

Opposite: Just hatched from its 2.5mm diameter egg, this tiny *Attacus atlas* larva is destined to become one of the largest moths in the world.

Above: The first moult takes place just four days after hatching.

The Giant Atlas Moth, *Attacus atlas*, from the family Saturniidae, one of the world's largest moths, is a wonderful example of extremes. The tiny black and white larvae emerge from orange-peel textured eggs of around 2.5mm diameter.

In all Lepidoptera the duration of each instar can vary greatly. The most important factors for development are temperature and availability of food, which it is probably fair to say, are of equal importance. Insects need to be warm enough for their metabolisms to function, so even if a caterpillar is sitting right in the middle of enough food for a lifetime, too low a temperature will prevent it from having sufficient energy to eat at all. For tropical or sub-tropical species such as the Giant Atlas Moth from Asia, temperature is less of an issue and they feed at an astonishing rate. The first moult occurs within three or four days of hatching and the second-instar larva has lost its dark hairs and gained longer spiny protrusions. At this stage the larva begins to develop a fine powdery coating.

Above: Beneath the powdery coating, the second instar larvae appear slightly more pink.

Right: By the third instar, the larvae have changed colour completely and are almost unrecognisable.

It is only a further four or five days before its next moult and despite the powdery coat, it is clear to see that in the third-instar larva, its original pinky hue has completely disappeared. Now nearly 50mm in length, it has changed completely, becoming greeny-blue, darkly speckled and considerably fatter.

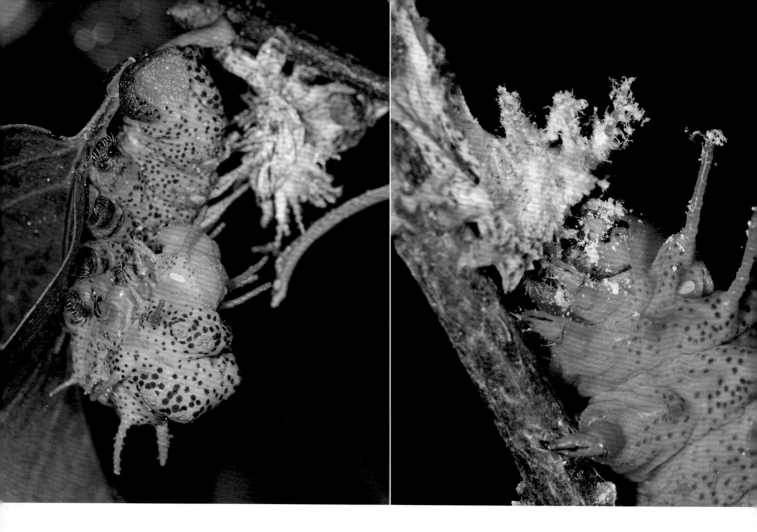

Nine days pass before the fourth instar is revealed and the true colours are easy to see before the fresh coat of powder forms. Now it has a vibrant coat of green and blue, with brown speckles all over and red oval discs on its claspers.

Seen here, common in many species of Lepidoptera is the practice of eating the exuvia. A lot of energy goes into making the skin, so it makes sense that a new instar's first meal will be to recover the cast-off source of nutrients. With *Attacus atlas* caterpillars, the white powder makes this an endearingly messy affair.

The later instar larvae devour leaves with breathtaking speed and as they get bigger, so the time between moults grows longer. In a little less than two weeks, this individual has grown to more than 80mm in length and is ready to shed its skin

Above: Recycling valuable protein by consuming their shed skin is a common practice in many species.

Right: Two days later and the powder coating has returned, emphasising the dark spots and creating an even more exotic appearance.

Left: Not long after moulting, the fifth instar is yet to regain its powdery coating.

Above: The cocoon is surprisingly small, just half the size of the mature caterpillar.

once again. The fifth and final instar is an impressive creature, looking as if it would be more at home sitting on a mushroom and smoking a hookah. Appetite unrelenting, it continues to eat for almost a further three weeks and grows to an even more impressive size. Reports of the sizes of *Attacus atlas* caterpillars vary a great deal with lengths averaging around 90mm. This individual reaches a little over 110mm in length before finally, feeding stops as pupation approaches.

Cocoons are spun amongst leaves on the host plant and depending on diet, can vary from dark brown to white or any shade in between. A truly remarkable aspect in the pupation of many saturniid moths is that these huge caterpillars manage to fit themselves into silk cocoons which are usually tiny in comparison with their own body length. At just 50mm long, the cocoon shown above must have been a tight squeeze before the pupa developed.

When the wings have had time to expand and harden, the adult *Attacus atlas* is as beautiful as it is huge.

Five weeks pass before the adult moth emerges and it is not just its size which is so remarkable. No trace remains of the blue-green goliath. In its place, with a wingspan of nearly 26 centimetres, is a heavy-bodied moth adorned with a complex pattern of reds, whites and golds.

Once emerged, the lifespans of adult silk moths are short. Males will survive for about a week, females up to ten days.

The fourth-instar caterpillar (left) moults once more and immediately consumes the exuvia.

The Indian Moon Moth, *Actias selene*, is another of the saturniid silk moths which illustrates many of the family's similarities and ultimate differences.

The first few weeks of life (previous page) take the caterpillar from a red hatchling with a black saddle, through a red second instar with no saddle, to a yellowy-green third instar covered in orange spikes and protrusions. The moult from fourth to fifth instar reveals how the head capsule, still hanging from tangled hairs, is shed quite separately from the rest of the exuvia. Once again, the moult is not wasted and is eaten immediately.

Left: Weaving its cocoon, the caterpillar's orange spots are still visible through the strands of silk. Development from pre-pupa into pupa may take up to a week.

Above: Saturniid pupae appear much more robust than those of butterflies.
  Although darker, the adult features can still be clearly discerned.

As with the Giant Atlas Moth, it will be around four or five weeks before the adult *Actias selene* emerges.

Although *Actias selene* larvae can grow as big or even bigger than those of *Attacus atlas*, the emerging adult is actually considerably smaller. With a wingspan of around 11 centimetres, the moth is no less beautiful.

In contrast with the Giant Atlas Moth, the Indian Moon Moth has retained a subtle version of its youthful colour. In common however, is that it too will only live for seven or eight days.

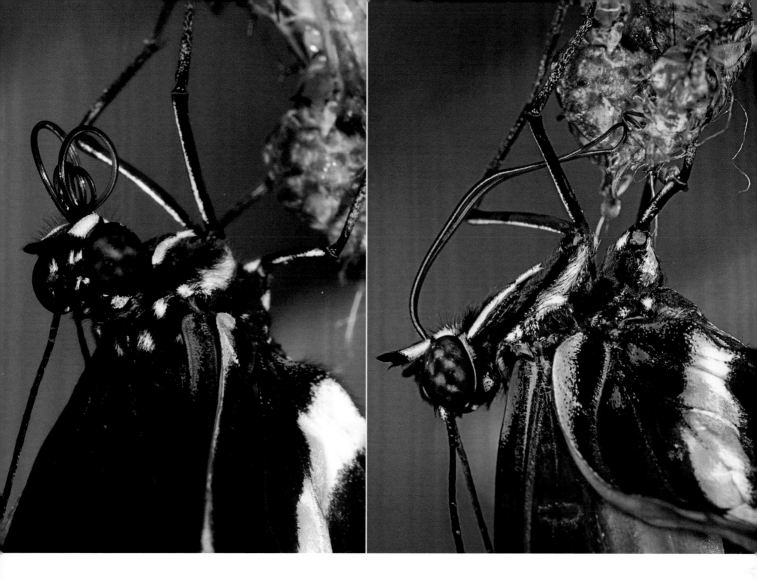

A newly emerged *Heliconius* butterfly from
South America will spend a little time wrestling
with its complex mouthparts to convert them
into the familiar feeding tube.

From bugs to beetles and fleas to flies, all adult insects have extremely complex mouthparts. One aspect is more clearly visible in Lepidoptera than any other order and that is how the ability to feed may be far from straightforward.

These different views of a *Heliconius* butterfly show that, as well as pumping fluids into the wings, it must also straighten out the two halves of its proboscis, known as maxillae, in order to bring them neatly together to form a tube through which it can drink. Each maxilla is coated with hooks and spines which connect the two sides together tightly. This individual appeared to go through the process a number of times over 30 minutes or so before being satisfied and coiling it into place.

HYMENOPTERA

Wasps, bees, ants and their relatives

Hymenoptera, meaning membrane-winged, is a vast order of insects second only to Coleoptera, with around 200,000 known species worldwide. They vary in size from the minuscule fairy flies (Mymaridae), some as small as 0.2mm, to huge spider-hunting wasps of the genus *Pepsis* which can reach a body length of around 40mm and wingspans around 100mm. I have rarely been as horrified as the first time I saw one of these enormous wasps in the jungles of northern Colombia, dragging a paralysed tarantula away to its burrow where it would lay a single egg on the hapless spider's abdomen. The living food supply would form the emerging wasp larva's entire source of nutrition through to adulthood.

The social species of bees, ants and wasps are considered to be the most highly evolved of all insects. Certainly, some of them display astonishingly complex levels of interaction and communication, to the extent that we can only wonder what must be going on inside their tiny brains.

The mining bee *Halictus marginatus* (opposite) maintains the same nest over a five- or six-year period. The colony as a whole may include hundreds of nests, all self-contained but constructed in close proximity to each other. In early spring, females emerge to repair and rebuild the chimneys of soil which lead down into the nests. Then, after a period of hectic feeding and larder-stocking, the nests are sealed and all activity returns underground. In autumn, the males emerge and spend a period of time foraging before entering other nests within the colony to mate with the females underground. By the end of autumn, the males stop flying, and once again the nests become quiet. Five or six months pass before the females emerge again to repeat the cycle, each year building a slightly taller chimney.

Opposite: Female mining bees of the species *Halictus marginatus* rebuilding the chimney-like structure over the nest, a job they repeat each spring when they emerge from a winter underground. The colony may grow to include hundreds of nests and thousands of individuals.

Above: One of the more familiar hymenopteran faces, a paper wasp drinks from a pool of water.

Above: Some ichneumons, such as this *Dolichomitus*, are capable of drilling their ovipositors into wood to lay their eggs inside beetle larvae.

Right: A *Colletes cunicularius* sporting pollen bearing pollinia which were glued to its face by an orchid.

Although the social bees and wasps may be the most familar, the vast majority of hymenopterans are solitary creatures living a huge diversity of lifestyles. Many, such as the ichneumon above, are parasitoid and exploit a wide variety of hosts. Unlike parasites, parasitoids are only parasitic for part of their life cycle and whereas parasites depend upon the host's good health, parasitoids' victims never survive. More on this later.

Not all the solitary species exploit other insects, in fact it is often they who are exploited. This ground-dwelling bee (right) *Colletes cunicularius* has been tricked into trying to mate with a bee orchid and will carry these pollinia to the next alluring orchid it finds along the way.

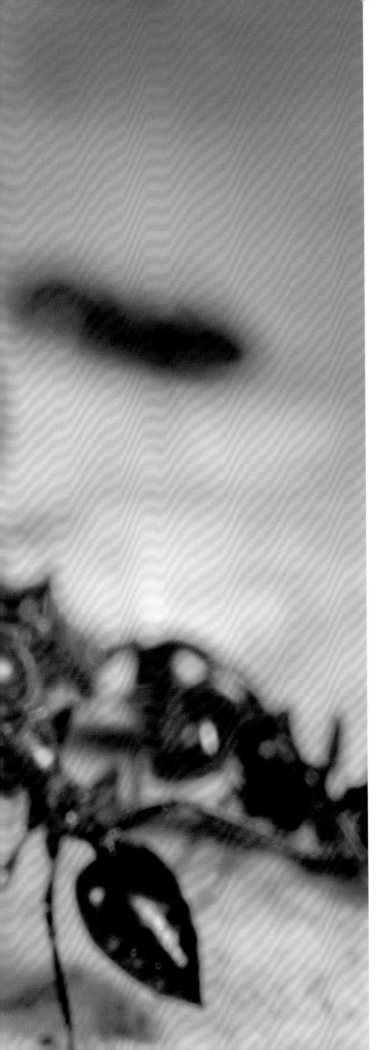

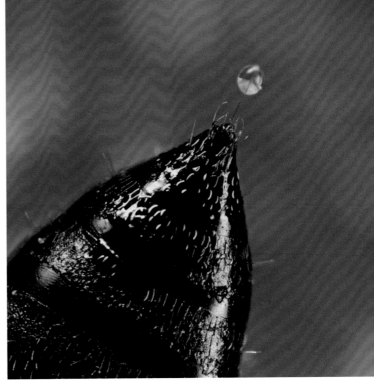

Left and above: Unlike that produced by the majority of hymenopterans, *Crematogaster* venom is topical rather than injected and individuals may brandish droplets as a threat. If threats go unheeded, they will apply the venom directly onto their attackers, or flick the droplets at them.

Ants are amongst the most sophisticated of social insects. There are around 12,000 species worldwide. From peaceful farmers to warring carnivores, soldiers, slaves and herders of aphids, sometimes ants seem to mirror humanity, the biggest differences being number of legs and that we think we're clever.

In the photograph to the left, a group of *Crematogaster scutellaris* are butchering the dried-out body of a worm. Threatened by my close proximity, one individual climbed onto the highest point to brandish a drop of venom from her sting.

Above: Ant larvae are constantly cleaned and tended to prevent any build-up of mould or mildew.

Below: The milky white early pupa (*Crematogaster* sp.) will darken gradually as maturity approaches.

Rearing of young within ant colonies involves non-stop care of the helpless larvae. Nursery workers will constantly clean the young to prevent the build-up of mildew or mould and ensure the good health of the brood. If weather conditions such as flooding pose a threat, the larvae will be carried to safer territory within the nest.

The final process of pupation reveals an interesting variable between certain species.

Above: Almost fully developed, a more mature pupa is being moved by a nursery worker.

Below: Unlike *Crematogaster*, pupae of the Yellow Meadow Ant, *Lasius flavus*, develop within papery pupal cases.

Some, such as *Crematogaster* (opposite below and above) pupate naked in the brood chamber. Others, such as the Yellow Meadow Ant, *Lasius flavus*, construct papery pupal cases which look like fat, pinkish grains of rice with a black spot on one end. Despite the added layer of protection, the developing pupae are tended with just as much care and attention as their naked cousins.

After heavy rain a queen *Polistes gallicus* tends to each of the nest's flooded cells in turn, meticulously sucking out the water and spitting it away from her vulnerable eggs and larvae.

Left: *Polistes gallicus* eggs, just half a millimetre in diameter, are laid one in each cell as it is completed, sometimes with a globule of a honey-like substance, probably left as a food supply.

Right: Laid just days apart, the staggered development of the larvae is clear to see.

The parenting behaviour displayed by some wasps is truly extraordinary and few more so than the paper wasps. In *Polistes gallicus*, shown here, the queen wakes from hibernation in the spring and builds a small vertical nest containing up to 40 cells. In each of these she will lay a single egg which will hatch in about two weeks. At this point the queen will begin to fly out on hunting missions, macerating her prey to feed to each hungry mouth. The eggs develop slightly after each other because they are laid individually as each cell is completed. In the photograph above left, the tiny eggs all appear to be the same (the globules visible in the lower cells are probably left as food supplies but it is far from certain why these are not deposited with every egg). The picture above right was taken two weeks later and it is clear to see how the larvae develop. The eggs in the cells shown here were laid just a day apart yet the difference in their development is dramatic.

After heavy rain, if the cells become flooded the queen will work quickly and tirelessly, sucking out the water and spitting it away from her vulnerable larvae.

When the weather is too hot, she will fan her wings over the cells to keep the larvae cool, moving around the nest to ensure that each larva is tended. Only occasionally will she take a brief rest, usually spent in the shade on the back of the nest. As the larvae mature, the difference between instars becomes completely undiscernable.

The larvae pass through five instars in three to four weeks. At this point they seal off the cell opening and enter their pre-pupal stage. Pupation then takes a further three weeks, during which time the queen will continue to tend and cool the nest, to bring the later larvae safely to maturity.

Above: As the larvae mature, any morphological differences become undiscernable.

Opposite: In another display of parental care, when the weather becomes too hot, the queen will move around the nest, fanning her wings to keep the larvae cool.

Above: Each emerging adult immediately joins the queen in tending and feeding.

Below: A mud dauber wasp, *Sceliphron caementarium*, collects a ball of mud for nest-building.

When the adults emerge, they all join together in tending and developing the nest, each sharing the tasks of feeding and fanning. Over the ensuing summer months the nest will continue to grow and may double in size, remaining busy until autumn.

In total contrast to the parental care of *Polistes*, the mud daubing wasps are solitary insects which expend a great deal of energy in providing for their offspring, but once a nest is complete and an egg is laid, the mother leaves it to its fate. The

Above: Gripping the ball with her jaws, she will apply the mud and return for more within minutes.

Below: The pots of *Sceliphron curvatum* make it easy to see when a wasp has begun to collect mud from a new location.

genus *Sceliphron* includes around 30 species, each of which builds nests of mud in various forms from pots to tubes and in numbers from half a dozen to thirty or more.

Sceliphron curvatum is a spider specialist. Females build rows or clusters of pots, each of which they pack with a larder of paralysed spiders. In each pot, a single egg is laid on the abdomen of one spider, the pot then sealed and the larva left to its own devices.

Above: Less than a millimetre long, the first instar sucks the innards from the living spider.

Left: Pots vary from 20 to 30 millimetres in length and contain a larder of around 20 paralysed spiders.

The pot (left) measures 20mm in length (the visible opening is 8mm across) and contains around 20 paralysed, but very much alive spiders. It may be of interest to note that on one occasion I emptied out and kept the contents of a pot. After roughly two weeks, some of the spiders started to move again, so it seems possible that the venom is effective just long enough for the paralysis to last through the feeding period.

Although any movement is imperceptible, the first-instar larva (above) has started to suck the innards out of the living spider.

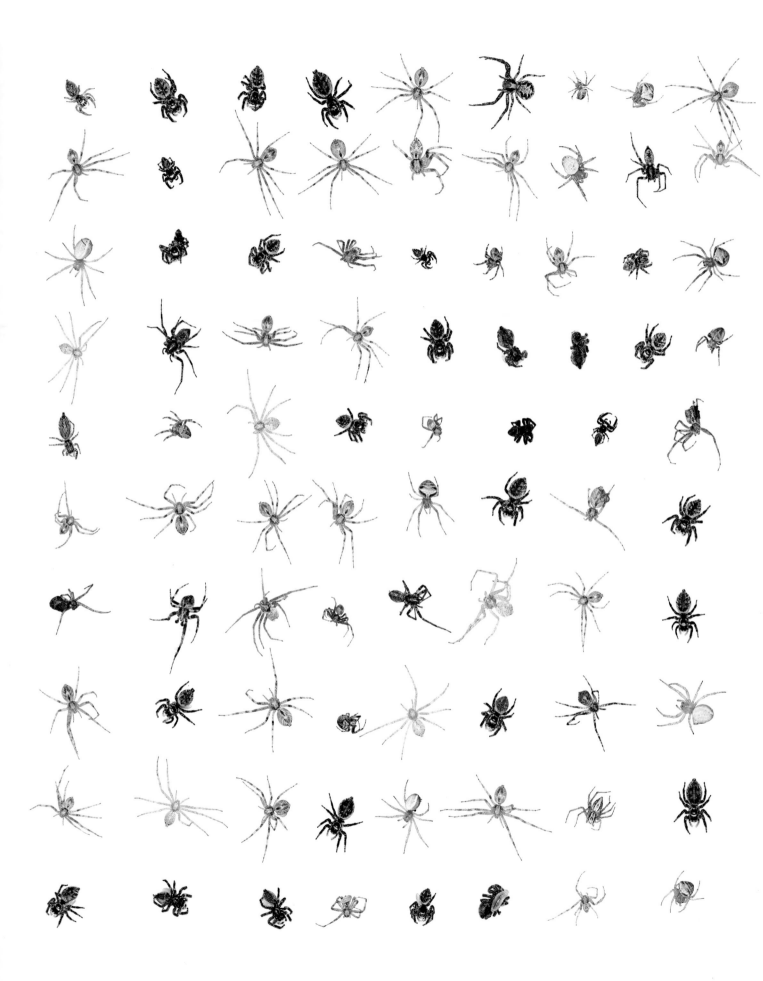

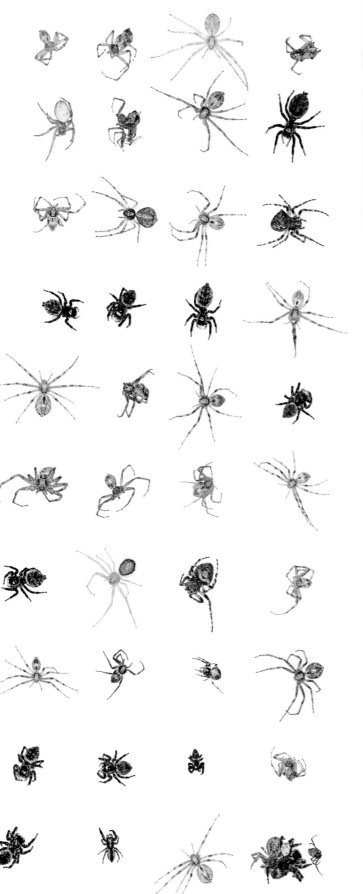

Above: In less than 24 hours the larva has doubled in size.

Left: The contents of a small nest of just eight pots gives some idea of the vast numbers of spiders consumed by this species.

Examining the contents of a nest of eight pots reveals that the choice of spiders is far from random. The majority of the 120 or so victims are fatter-bodied females and many are salticids where both sexes are more plump and juicy.

Within 24 hours the tiny larva has already doubled in size and the spider's abdomen is visibly losing volume.

Above: On day four, the larva is in mid-moult with no apparent pause in feeding

Below: On day six, another moult can just be seen. The grub has released the empty spider and will soon latch on to another.

By day four (above) the first spider's abdomen is now little more than an empty bag and the larva is in the process of a moult (the skin can be seen peeling ventrally). The mouth-parts are much more developed by day six (left). At this stage it has moved on to solids and is eating the spiders in their entirety. It may seem surprising that another moult is beginning so soon (the skin can be seen peeling along the larva's stomach) but in fact they

Above: Growth can be so rapid that moults may occur within 24 hours of each other. This and the photograph below left are separated by just 18 hours.

Below: As the final instar approaches pupation, its body takes on a yellow hue.

can grow so quickly that some moults take place well within 24 hours of each other, as can be seen in the photograph from day seven (above) taken just 18 hours later.

In the later stages of the final instar, just scraps of spider carcasses remain. As pupation approaches, the larva's speckled and glistening body acquires a more transluscent yellow appearance.

Replaced in its pot for scale, what began life as a sub-millimetre grub has grown, almost to fill its now empty pot. After less than two weeks of continuous messy eating, fragments of spiders' legs cling to its body making it seem slightly hairy. The overall shape has refined quite considerably, its head, once a fifth of the overall length, now appears as little more than a tiny capsule on its swollen body.

Finally it begins to draw silken threads around itself, secreted from salivary glands in the mouth. It is only really in this process of spinning its pupal case that the true flexibility of this larval morphology becomes apparent.

Above: Ready to pupate, it begins to draw silken threads around itself.

Opposite: Just 12 days after beginning to suck on its first spider, the larva's enormous rate of growth is clear to see.

Placed into a glass test tube with the same internal dimensions as its pot, the pupa continues developing completely normally. With the construction of the pupal case now visible, the process, from left to right, shows that the pupa first produces relatively coarse fibres to create a sort of framework to support the delicate transparent film in which it will seal itself. Despite the constraints of such a confined space, the pupa is sufficiently flexible to twist itself repeatedly from head to tail, making sure that the structure is even throughout.

When the framework is complete, the pupa secretes a different liquid, creating the smooth, dark walls of its cocoon. From start to finish, the structure takes a full 24 hours to complete. One week later, the adult shape is beginning to develop.

Above: Twisting repeatedly up and down, construction of the cocoon takes a full 24 hours.

Far right: One week after completing the cocoon, the adult body shape is beginning to develop. It will be nearly a further two weeks before the adult emerges.

The shedding of the final skin frees the adult, allowing it to move and cut its way through the top of the clay pot. The caps are always thinner than the walls to make it easier for the adult to escape. In some wasp species, the emerging adult uses saliva to soften the clay before chewing its way out. Of those I have observed, there has been little consistency in behaviour on emerging. Some fly off immediately, others stay close to the pot for up to an hour. Either way, despite their effect on spider populations, *Sceliphron* are undeniably one of the most elegant and least aggressive of wasps.

Above: Just emerged from its pot, this *Sceliphron curvatum* adult shows the distinctive slender waist, called a pedicel.

Right: The adult emerges by chewing through the thin layer of clay at the top of the pot.

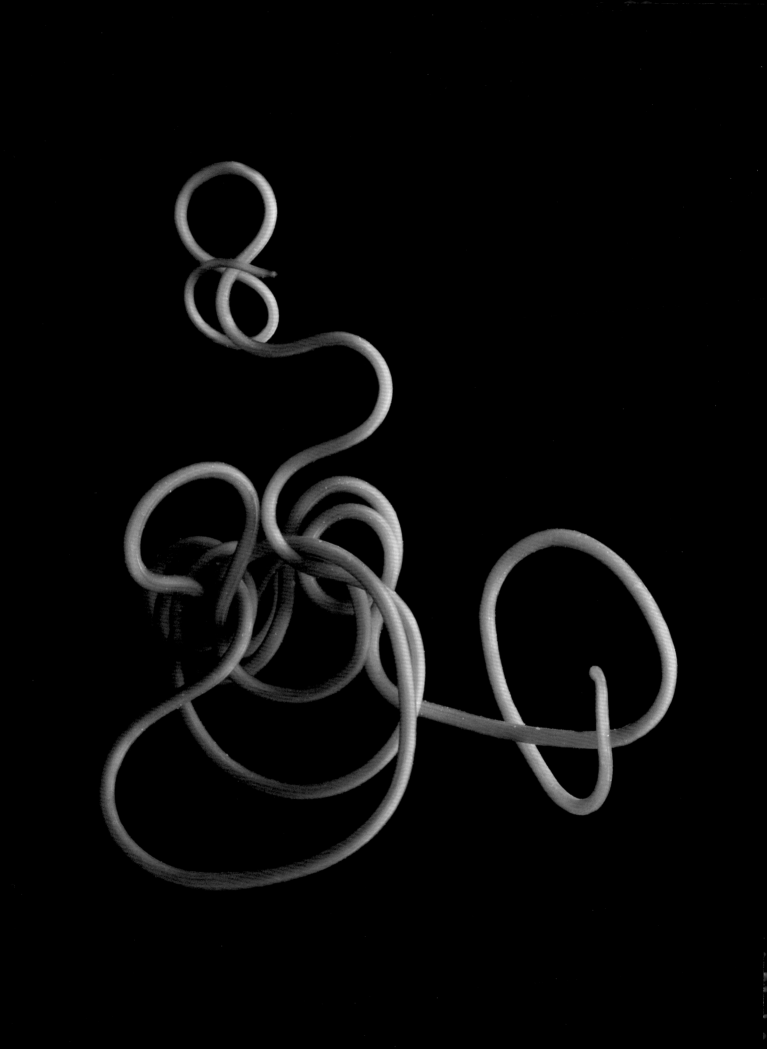

THE DARK SIDE

Not everything in the garden is rosy

The creature opposite is a Gordian worm. This specimen is one millimetre in diameter, almost a metre long, and it came out of a cricket. The most remarkable aspect of this creature's life cycle is not that something so long can grow inside a cricket, but that when it reaches maturity, it compels the cricket to kill itself by jumping into water, at which point the worm leaves its doomed host and swims away to find a mate. Mind control spreads far beyond the world of horror movies.

The potentially disturbing subject of parasites and parasitoids has arisen a few times throughout this book and it seems churlish not to delve a little deeper into the lives of these nightmarish creatures, if only very briefly. These marvels of evolution, whatever form they may take, have adapted to exploit every species on earth including each other. However unsavoury, we cannot escape the reality that parasitism is enormously successful, and that the insect world has far more than its fair share.

Left: A Violet Carpenter Bee infested with mites, all clustered at the thorax and feasting on haemolymph.

Above: An individual mite photographed between millimetre markings.

Opposite: A metre-long Gordian worm, not long exited from an ill-fated bush cricket.

237

Amongst the most common types of parasite are the mites. In the right conditions, these arachnids can reproduce quickly and reach plague-like numbers, as can be seen in the photograph opposite. With so many mites on board, this first-instar cricket is being drained of haemolymph and will not survive for long. The nymph below, with just a dozen or so passengers, was dead in 12 hours. To give a clearer sense of scale, the actual size is shown in the bottom left of the photograph. These mites are significantly smaller than the full stop at the end of this sentence.

However gruesome, there is at least a 'What you see is what you get' sort of aspect to mites. The creatures that seem so bewildering are the ones which have evolved lifestyles so seemingly impossible that it is hard to imagine how they became so successful. I struggle to understand how some wasps which parasitise other parasites can pin-point the exact position of an egg or larva which is already inside the body of a host. How does an ichneumon physically have the strength to drill its ovipositor into solid wood to place an egg inside a wood-boring larva? Have you ever tried just pushing a pin into a tree without needing a replacement thumb?

With all the myriad ways that have evolved simply as a means to survive, none can be as chilling as the real-life zombies. Some of the biggest perpetrators of fatal mind control are braconid wasps. Around 20,000 different species are known to science, and the true number may be at least double. All of them are parasitoids; whatever they exploit will die.

Opposite: A first-instar cricket nymph besieged by mites, all sucking the life out of it. Certain death is only hours away.

Right: Another first instar with far fewer passengers died within a day. Actual size is shown in the bottom left corner of the photograph.

Right: A doomed Black-veined White caterpillar, parasitised by braconid wasps. Having spun a protective web around their cocoons, it will guard them until they emerge, unless it dies of starvation first.

The species *Cotesia glomerata* specializes in pierid butterflies like the Black-veined White caterpillar above. The adult wasp stabs a caterpillar with its ovipositor and lays around 20 eggs directly inside its body. When the eggs hatch, the larvae feed inside their host but avoid any vital organs to ensure that it stays alive – for now.

After about two weeks of feeding on the unfortunate host, when the larvae are approaching pupation they chew their way out through the caterpillar's skin and spin cocoons on the closest plant stem. When all the wasp larvae are safely inside their cocoons, the caterpillar spins a protective

web around the cluster, which it then protects as if its own life depended on it. The control is so complete that the caterpillar does not feed, remaining curled protectively around its charge. Now no more than a constant guard, the caterpillar wards off any approaching threat with aggressive swaying movements. This behaviour continues tirelessly until the caterpillar dies of starvation which may or may not be before the adult wasps emerge.

It is impossible to put a percentage on the number of insects within any given species which are parasitised each year, but for any parasite to have evolved successfully, the number must be significant. On many occasions,

Above: A scelionid wasp emerges from a shield bug egg.

Right: A braconid wasp emerging from a *Pieris brassicae* chrysalis. An interesting illustration of the hard-wired behaviour of these creatures is that of the 20 or so wasps that emerged from this chrysalis, they all either chewed a fresh exit hole, or chewed around the edge of an existing one. Not one just climbed out without chewing, despite the fact that, after wasp number six, there were already holes with almost enough space to exit without even touching the sides.

I have waited weeks to photograph larvae hatching from their eggs, or sometimes months for an overwintering butterfly to emerge from its chrysalis in the spring, only to find that the occupants have been tiny wasps.

Perhaps, when it comes to the natural world, the only thing we can say with any certainty is that we should always expect the unexpected.

PHOTOGRAPHING
INSECTS

Also known as 'The Art of Waiting'

A question I am asked quite often is: 'Why insects?' With all the cute and cuddly stuff out there, why focus on creepy crawlies? I usually say, hopefully without sounding too pompous, that whilst some may creep, they never crawl and up close and personal many of them are extremely cute. On top of that, there's many a human who could learn some parenting skills from the likes of earwigs and social wasps. The thing is, the entire natural world fascinates and enthralls to pretty much the same degree, it's just that insects seldom let you down. The greater part of a nature photographer's life is waiting. You can sit for days and weeks, waiting to photograph a particular event, and all the time, insects will put on a show to keep you company, although admittedly this won't apply to marine photographers.

Above left: *Saitis barbipes* with prey (I know it's not an insect). This jumping spider waves its enlarged third legs in a semaphore-like courtship display. How anyone could fail to find either of the above creatures cute is beyond me.

Above: *Phymata crassipes* (family Reduviidae). I may never have seen this tiny bug had I not been waiting two weeks for a cricket to get lucky.

From a personal perspective, being an insect-lover is like being a kid in a sweet shop. So many discoveries still to be made and, oh my goodness, which way to turn? It is no exaggeration to say that almost every day of my life I see a species I don't recognise and I assure you it is not because I have a lousy memory. The only downside is that sometimes it can take weeks to identify an obscure species of something so small, it needs to be squinted at through a lens in the first place. How often has something tiny flown past your nose and been all but ignored? Yet it could have been one of the many aliens in our midst. I have to confess that I drive my wife quietly potty when, in the middle of a conversation, I might leap up to check something that has just popped into view. There is no discourtesy attached, simply that the thought always crosses my mind that I may never have seen one of those before and equally may not do so again. The important thing is to take nothing for granted, even in the most familiar of situations. It is an inescapable fact that generally speaking, the best place to discover a new species is wherever you happen to be right now, although that is hopefully not the case if you are reading this in a restaurant.

The single most important rule of nature photography is that your work should never, ever cause suffering (photographer's self-inflicted pain doesn't count). This includes causing stress, or anything else which might cause the subject to behave abnormally. Aside from ethics, you learn nothing of a creature's behaviour if you only observe it under adverse or constrained conditions.

I cannot deny that there have been numerous occasions during the three years of making this book when my resilience has been truly tested. When planning the section on Diptera, I wanted to illustrate at least one species with an aquatic larval stage. I didn't really mind what it was, just so long as I could shoot the life cycle, so what I needed to create was a genuinely natural environment that could be moved into controlled conditions when necessary. The greatest limitation of extreme macro photography is that depth of field, or the amount that can be held in focus, can be measured in tenths of millimetres. It is hard enough when the subject itself is moving, and utterly impossible to focus at all if even the gentlest breeze causes the water surface to move as well.

These insects lay their eggs in water or damp soil and can remain in dry conditions for long periods waiting for rain to return. So I cut a number of small turfs, put them in plastic containers and then just left them alone for six months. As the weeks passed, over and over again the containers flooded in heavy rain and dried out in the heat of the sun. It is bizarre what can excite a man on a mission, but I confess to a sense of euphoria the first day I found a pot heaving with tiny larvae. After that it was a simple matter of keeping them topped up with rain water and maintaining a watchful eye as much as possible. At any one time I was observing around a dozen different

The mini set-up for mosquitoes and midges. The container holds a waterlogged turf which was left outdoors for six months to allow anything to lay their eggs. The background photograph of leaves creates more natural reflections on the water surface. The blue base is a potter's wheel which can be rotated to change the viewing angle, without needing to move the lighting.

species and, far too many times, something happened behind my back whilst I was photographing something else.

The photograph above shows the set-up for the mosquito and midge photographs. I spent some time just sitting by a puddle in the woods, watching how the light played and seeing how the surrounding foliage affected the reflections. I then took a photograph of the brambles and ivy which I positioned over the larvae. Actually, the trickiest part of this whole set-up was finding exactly the right combination of angles between the slope of the picture and the position of the flash which would be creating the reflections on the water surface.

It all worked reasonably well, the only downside was that over the months it took to capture the entire sequence, the studio became a haven for mosquitoes and midges. Being the only mammal in the studio, I was dinner for every single one of them and had to keep reminding myself whose stupid idea this had been in the first place. I released as many as possible but many refused to leave, probably having learned that, in the not too distant future, the only mammal in the room would once again be looking through a camera and exposing a suitably juicy neck.

Obviously, photographing a book about metamorphosis with the intention of capturing hatchings and moults, meant more watching and waiting than actually taking photographs. Normally, the sense of achievement at getting a shot after months of planning and waiting, is enough of a mental carrot to dangle in front of an increasingly weary photographer. I confess that my own Zen-like patience was tested to the limits when photographing the sequence on antlions. How do you know when something that lives in the soil is going to climb out? Answer: You don't. Well, you have a very rough idea. From stopping pit-building to making a cocoon is about a week. From constructing the cocoon to actual emergence is about four weeks. From a get-the-shot point of view that means, start watching at week three and be prepared to wait until the end of week five... and they are nocturnal. To cut a long story short, I didn't go to bed for five weeks one summer and four weeks the following year. I still didn't get the shot I wanted but I did, thank goodness, manage to capture the life cycle.

People often ask why I don't just use trip beams and technology to let the gear do the job. The principal reason is the depth of field issue. If a really tiny creature moves more than a millimetre or so away from my point of focus, I will not be happy with the result, and I would rather wait a month for the shot that I want, than not have to wait for the shot that I just happened to get. On top of that, you only truly learn about animals by watching them.

Without doubt, the most exciting thing to come out of this project is the section on the little-known Vermileonidae. How I came to photograph them in the first place is too long a story to write here, but basically I thought I was digging up antlion pits and ended up with a creature I knew nothing whatsoever about, which then took a full two months to identify. The photographs of the emerging adult (page 170) are a world first which came after two years of waiting. It was infuriating that it emerged facing away from the camera, but nevertheless, a totally new experience. To add to the euphoria of success, Vermileonidae tend to emerge around sunrise, so after all the waiting, it also meant I didn't have to get up before dawn again, at least for a while.

An empty vermileonid pupal case. This emerging adult forced itself vertically to the surface and climbed out through the thorax. A spectacular event that happened when my back was turned, photographing beetles.

For all the trials and tribulations there may be in working with wildlife, the unpredictable nature of all animals is what makes them so fascinating to watch and why it is so rewarding to gain a deeper understanding. It is, perhaps, a sad fact that none of us will ever live long enough to read every book that has ever been written, hear all the music ever recorded, see all the paintings painted or photographs taken. No matter how hard we might try there would always be more to experience. So it is with the whole of nature and insects in particular. Of the millions of species alive throughout the world today, even the most dedicated naturalist will only ever scrape the surface of the full richness of six-legged life on earth. That said, maybe it isn't really such a bad thing. All lovers of the natural world share one blessing in particular: we can never, ever be bored.

ACKNOWLEDGEMENTS

For making a difference, my grateful thanks go to:

First and foremost, Dr George McGavin: they broke the mould. Despite his own, often unrelenting workload, George always found the time to reply to my plaintive questions, no matter where he was in the world. Without his enthusiastic help, support, good humour and proof reading, not to mention his encyclopaedic knowledge, I would have stumbled down many a blind alley and lost far too much precious time along the way.

For her eternal support, my long-suffering wife Julie, who tends the garden lovingly, in the resigned acceptance that not far away, I am rearing all the things which eat it. Plus the fact that, being on almost constant critter watch for over three years, I have not taken her anywhere. I shall enjoy redressing the balance.

Cathie and Pascal Proust, owners of the delightful butterfly farm *Les Papillon d'Amarente* in the Ariège region of France, for letting me get under their feet and offering helpful advice. My sons Damien and Alex, and daughter-in-law Pam, for their constant interest in what I do, with particular thanks to Damien and Pam for their valuable input. My father for his enthusiasm and frequent gifts of captured insects. My sister Kate for helping to make life easier. Lisa Thomas at Bloomsbury Publishing, whose passion for the idea really helped to get the project off the ground and designer Nicola Liddiard for her patience and hard work in pulling it together.

Finally, and somewhat belatedly, my mother. Partly for my childhood visits to the Natural History Museum in London, but mostly for never screaming, 'Get that out of here!...' Except once when, aged about eight, I brought home a dead hedgehog, complete with evacuating army of fleas, most of which were already halfway to my elbows.

Rupert Soskin

BIBLIOGRAPHY

and further reading

Bwahane, G. P., Mamlayya, A. B., Koli, Y. J., Phonde, Y. A., Aland, S.R. and Gaikwad, S. M. (2011) Life History of *Attacus atlas* Linn. (Saturniidae: Lepidoptera) on Sapium insegne benth. From Western Ghats, Maharashtra. *The Bioscan* 6(3) 497-500

Chapman, R. F. (1998) *The Insects: Structure and Function, 4th Edition,* Cambridge University Press, Cambridge.

Chinery, M. (1986) *Collins Guide to Insects of Britain and Western Europe.* Collins, London.

Devetak, D. (2008) Wormlion *Vermileo vermileo* (L.) (Diptera: Vermileonidae) in Slovenia and Croatia. *Annales Ser. Hist. Nat.* 18 - 2008 - 2, 283-286.

Devetak, D. (2008) Substrate particle size-preference of wormlion Vermileo vermileo (Diptera: Vermileonidae) larvae and their interaction with antlions. *Eur. J. Entomol.* 105: 631-635.

Esperk, T., Tammaru, T. and Nylin, S. (2007) Intraspecific Variability in Number of Larval Instars in Insects. *Journal of Economic Entomology* 100 (3): 627-645.

Grimaldi, D. and Engel, M. S. (2006) *Evolution of the Insects,* Cambridge University Press, New York.

Heinrich, B. (1999) *The Thermal Warriors: Strategies of Insect Survival,* Harvard University Press, Massachusetts.

McGavin, G. C. (2011) *Essential Entomology, An Order-by-Order Introduction.* Oxford University Press, Oxford.

McGavin, G. C. (1999) *Bugs of the World*. Blandford, London.

Plateaux-Quenu, C. (1962) *Biology of Halictus marginatus Brulle. Jour Apicultural Res.* 1: 41-51

Prado, S. S., Rubinoff, D. and Almeida, R. P. P. (2006) Vertical Transmission of a Pentatomid Caeca-Associated Symbiont. *Entomological Society of America* 99 (3): 577-585.

Starnecker, G. and Hazel, W. (1999) Convergent evolution of neuroendocrine control of phenotypicplasticity in pupal colour in butterflies. *Proceedings of the Royal Society* B, London.

Tanaka, S. and Ohsaki, N. (2006) Behavioral manipulation of host caterpillars by the primary parasitoid wasp *Cotesia glomerata* (L.) to construct defensive webs against hyperparasitism. *Ecological Research* (Impact Factor: 1.51). 01/2006; 21(4):570-577.

Wigglesworth, V. B. (1984) *Insect Physiology*, Eighth Edition. Chapman and Hall, New York.

Wigglesworth, V. B. (1983) *Insect Hormones*, Oxford University Press.

INDEX